The Beauty That Remains

THE BEAUTY THAT REMAINS

A Vietnamese Refugee's Journey to Freedom

QUYNH DAO

heart books

First published by Heart Books in 2017

Copyright © Quynh Dao, 2017

All rights reserved. No part of this book may be reproduced or transmitted by any person or entity, including internet search engines or retailers, in any form or by any means, electronic or mechanical, including photocopying (except under the statutory exceptions provisions of the Australian *Copyright Act 1968*), recording, scanning or by any information storage and retrieval system without the prior written permission of Heart Books.

Heart Books
PO Box 237, Camberwell VIC 3124 Australia

A Cataloguing-in-Publication record for this book is available from the National Library of Australia

ISBN 978 0 9577482 3 1

All photos included in this book belong to the author.

To the memory of hundreds of thousands of Vietnamese Boat People who perished at sea on their journeys in search of freedom

An Introduction

The Beauty That Remains is the sequel to Quynh Dao's *Tales from a Mountain City*. It vividly describes the author's experience in a Malaysian refugee camp, where interviews with immigration officials and their subsequent acceptance would lead to a new life.

This is a moving story about people being suddenly thrust into a new place, a new culture and the mental adjustment needed to be able to move forward into another world. Readers will be touched by the author's feeling of gratitude for the welcome and the friendliness she received from the Australian people from the time she and her family stepped off the plane and were placed in a migrant hostel.

Hard work and perseverance has been the basis of success for the thousands of Vietnamese people who came to Australia. In these pages one is privileged to learn the difficult road to a new life in a new country.

Tamie Fraser AO

FOREWORD

In 1980, after several failed attempts, I made a successful escape by boat from communist Vietnam. I spent the next 16 months in a refugee camp in Malaysia and arrived in Melbourne in 1981. Australia opened its arms and heart to embrace refugees like me who came by the plane loads –and in some instances by the boat loads, too.

19 years of age at the time, I had my share of difficulties that most newly arrived migrants experience. I struggled with the English language. It took me some time to get used to Australian customs. Once a friend and I lined up for hours to watch a football match. As it turned out, they were playing the Aussie version and not the real football we had been brought up. We were the dumbest spectators that day at the G. (I've totally converted to Aussie Rules since). Another time, while at the pet food section of a supermarket, we were in awe at the row of tins, which we thought contained dog meat! We could not figure out what "bring a plate" meant on a community notice. These and many other things appeared strange to me who came from a small village in the countryside of South Vietnam. However what impressed me most was the kindness and the support that ordinary Australians had shown me and my family.

Being a former boat person is not the only thing that defines me, but there's no denying such an incredible experience has informed my views of the world and has shaped me into the person I am today.

When I was appointed Auxiliary Bishop of Melbourne in 2011, I chose 'Duc in altum', meaning 'Go out into the deep' as my motto.

It was my way to acknowledge my past as a boat person, to pay tribute to millions of Vietnamese who 'went out into the deep' sea in search of freedom following the communist takeover of South Vietnam in 1975, and to commemorate hundreds of thousands who perished at sea before reaching a safe haven.

In my Coat of Arms, the blue colour and the Southern Cross represents Australia, my new homeland that I love very much, that embraced refugees and migrants with compassion and generosity. It truly rose to the challenge during the boat people crisis.

It was that spirit of generosity from a compassionate world that had transformed the Vietnamese refugees' tragic story into a story of hope.

The Beauty That Remains is Quynh Dao's personal account of such wonderful transformation that many thousand former Vietnamese boat people and I are living witnesses.

The terrorist events of September 11, 2001 changed many people's perception about asylum seekers and refugees. Australia in the year 2016 does not seem to be as welcoming to them as it was in the 70's and 80's, despite the fact that displaced people are among the world's most pressing issues.

The successful settlement of the Vietnamese refugees, I think, is testament that a society galvanised by courage and compassion can rise to any humanitarian challenge.

Australia is what it is today largely because of the determination and drive for a better future on the part of migrants and refugees. We honour the legacy of this great nation not by excessive protectionism, isolation and defence of our privilege at all costs. Rather, we make it greater by our concern and care for asylum seekers in the spirit of compassion and solidarity that has marked the history of our country from its beginning.

Most Rev Vincent Long OFM Conv, Bishop of Parramatta and Australian Catholic Bishops Delegate for Migrants and Refugees

*I do not think of all the misery but of
the beauty that still remains.*
Anne Frank

AUTHOR'S NOTE

My name Quynh Dao (pronounced 'Quinn Dow') and the names of historic and public figures are real.

The names of members of my family, other individuals and some of their identification details have been changed for their safety and privacy.

English translation of Vietnamese and French texts is by the author unless otherwise referenced.

The Beauty That Remains is a sequel to *Tales from a Mountain City* A Vietnam War memoir. For those who have not read *Tales from a Mountain City,* the prologue provides the historical and social context that forms the backdrop of the story in this book.

PROLOGUE

I did not think that the sky would ever fall on my head but the day the Communists declared victory over South Vietnam, my country, on 30 April 1975, the ensuing devastation came close to Armageddon. The twenty-year war between the Communists in the North and the young liberal democracy in the South, known to the world as the Vietnam War, had ended. I was fifteen years old at the time.

My family lived in Dalat, a mountainous city situated three hundred kilometres north of Saigon, South Vietnam's capital. It was built by the French when they were our colonial masters. It possessed the beauty and charm of a French provincial town. Lush pine trees and Japanese cherry trees bearing pinkish flowers were its trademarks.

Living in a country at war, peace was a fervent dream in every Vietnamese heart. Yet it remained elusive the day the fighting ended. Innocent people caught in the turmoil of war found themselves thrown into a different kind of strife – the turmoil of peace.

The Communists wasted no time in imposing their authoritarian way over their newly conquered territory.

Over one million former soldiers, civil servants and teachers of the vanquished regime were rounded up and sent to the dreaded 're-education' camps. They were branded American lackeys, reactionaries, enemies of the revolution who had the blood of the people on their hands. Their families were stigmatized and referred to by a generic term – 'of tainted background'.

South Vietnamese business and manufacturing owners, industry leaders, producers of goods and services, even the humble small traders who worked hard all their lives to earn a living were suddenly told they had committed a grave sin against humanity: they were branded capitalists, enemies of the state. Those identified as undesirable in this new social paradigm were banished to the New Economic Zones - wild and desolate places in the middle of nowhere, the Vietnamese Siberia. With only few personal belongings, they were left to fend for themselves against nature and wild beasts. Many lost their lives there.

There was supposedly no more class in the progressive society of the Socialist Republic of Vietnam, however there were social categories, fifteen of them in all. The crème-de-la-crème were families of revolutionary background. They occupied the top tier. Their children only needed seven marks to pass the university entrance examination papers. Families of former South Vietnamese army personnel ranked second last. Their children needed twenty one marks to get into university, three times the marks required for Communist nobility. When their father or brother was released from re-education camp, years later, their status would go up one notch, to thirteenth place. Those unlucky enough to have been born in families branded reactionary and anti-revolutionary stayed at the very bottom of the list. They might as well give up hope for a place at university, or any place at all in society.

The working class was elevated to the pedestal of society's most progressive element at the forefront of the country's advancement to socialism. The Party and the revolutionary government declared themselves the wise leader and representative of the working class, and took up the task of assuming total control of properties and people on their behalf. This meant they could do whatever they wanted with people's possessions and their lives.

My father was spared prison because he had retired from the civil service ten years before. However my family was kicked out of our own home because a group of Communist soldiers wanted to occupy it. A family friend came to our rescue and opened her house to us, otherwise we would have joined the new homeless, decent people who were thrown out of their own homes at the arbitrary order of the new ruler of the land. We would eventually be allowed to return to our home, even though it would now be just an empty shell. When they moved out, the soldiers took with them anything that caught their fancy.

Food and basic necessities that were abundant in the South, even in war time, disappeared, while the magic of communist common ownership in peace time never manifested.

Books were burned. Poets, writers, journalists, musicians, literary translators, movie producers and publishers were locked up. In the former free and open society of South Vietnam, these people had the right to speak their minds and express what they felt. The new authorities saw them as potential troublemakers. Many monks and priests also ended up in prison. Their faiths put them under immediate suspicion. It was obvious that their loyalty did not lie with Uncle Ho and the Party.

People were disappearing without any trace. No reason was given and no one dared to ask. The hope of rebuilding the war-torn country in the spirit of goodwill and reconciliation had all but vanished. An atmosphere of fear reigned.

PART I
THE SOUTH SEA ANGELS

October 1978
It had been three years since the fall of Saigon. I turned eighteen, finished high school and had just moved to Saigon to start my undergraduate course at the French faculty of Saigon University.

My place in the new society was inauspicious.

Every person was required to fill a Declaration of Personal Background, a detailed questionnaire that sought information about the declarer, his parents, siblings, paternal and maternal grandparents, and paternal and maternal cousins. For each person within that three-generation family tree, the government wanted to know their date of birth, their present and past occupations, and present and past activities, making clear these were pro- or anti-revolutionary. All Declarations of Personal Background required certification by the cadres in charge of several layers of the new bureaucracies, including the neighbourhood chief, the chief of the local quarter and the district chief.

Mine carried the following verdict, signed and stamped at the bottom of the last page, in red ink: 'Certifying that the declarer's father is a former official of the lackey government and the declarer's family lives in a two thousand square metre property.' I would wear this tag, as ominous as the

Star of David that Jews were forced to wear in Nazi-occupied areas, wherever I went, in whatever I did, when I applied for anything, be it a travel permit, university entrance or hospital admission, for the rest of my life.

I would like to think that my success at gaining a place at university was thanks to my hard work and my ability, as I had always been a top student at school. However the rules had changed. It was hard to admit that I might just be lucky this time. Whoever looked at my application for university entrance might happen to be a fair-minded person who disregarded my background and marked my exam paper based purely on merit. Needless to say, I preferred such objective and reliable assessment criteria.

I shared a small flat in Saigon with my older siblings - brother Tin, sister Ba, and stepsister My. Tin was in his second year at the University of Economics, a nice name for a dumping ground for those who could not get into any other universities for a variety of reasons. Tin always did well at high school. In all likelihood he could have got a place at the School of Medicine or the prestigious Phu Tho Polytechnic University, if not for the local cadre's damning comments in his Declaration of Personal Background: 'Certifying that the declarer is of lackey background and his family lives in a two thousand square metre property. It is proposed that his application for university entrance not be considered.' There were many Communist soldiers in his class. They were not academically inclined but had fought well in the battlefield. A place at the University of Economics was their reward. The government needed a large number of personnel to create a new league of cadres trained in the new school of thoughts to reshape the South Vietnamese economy. Students at the University of Economics learned the political and economic theory of socialism and Marxism-Leninism, and the Party's directives. At the graduation ceremony, graduates would have to swear their unswerving loyalty to the Party.

My sister Ba graduated with a teaching degree in French. She was assigned to a far-flung place in the countryside. My stepsister My had already finished a business degree before the Communist takeover but her qualification was now worthless. Tertiary qualifications in law, business and humanities from South Vietnamese universities were not recognised by the new regime. The content of these courses had been based on the premises of the rule of law, the separation of powers, a market economy and freedom of thoughts. These were now considered irrelevant, reactionary in nature, even dangerous and subversive. My stepsister had to retrain by completing a two-year diploma course at the University of Economics, which got her a job weighing vegetables at a collectivised farm. The back-breaking work was too much for her tiny frame. My mother had to bribe a cadre who procured her an office job at a construction company. Her task was to make copies of building plans by hand; in other words, she performed the function of a photocopy machine, not available in Communist Vietnam at the time. Fluent in French, My had hoped to work as an interpreter for a small team of French consultants at the company. A scant number of foreigners were allowed into the country after the war to help revive some industries. Our family's tainted background worked against her.

We were part of the majority of the South Vietnamese population whom the authorities considered as workhorses - usable, readily disposable and not to be trusted. The power and the privileges, including placements at top universities and plum jobs in the big cities, were for members of the Party and Ho Chi Minh's Youth Group, the equivalent of Mao's Red Guards. Talent and intelligence were irrelevant. The 'tainted' learned to accept their lowly status in this heaven for the proletariat. Many South Vietnamese doctors, teachers and university lecturers either spent years in labour camps or were unemployed because they failed the personal background test. My former literature teacher now scraped a living as a porter at a bus depot. My French teacher, a Catholic nun, was no longer allowed to teach.

I had not exactly looked forward to my relocation to Saigon. Except for some short trips, this was the first time that I ever lived away from my parents and my hometown. Already I missed Dalat's tranquility and cool climate. Saigon's endless crowds and its unbearable heat were a mammoth personal test for me. I had no idea that challenges one hundred times, one thousand times harder than this were waiting for me. My life was about to change forever.

* * *

One afternoon when I came home from university, my brother Tin, half-serious, half-flippant, said, 'Quynh, you won't have to go to lectures tomorrow.'

'How come? I still have another week of Political Education to go,' I said.

'Well, sister, if you want to stay for the Political Education, that's up to you. But we're going.'

Going. Everybody was going—anywhere, by any means— because however frightening the unknown might be, surely it could not be as suffocating and soul-crushing as the kind of life we were all being forced to lead?

'If the electricity poles had legs, they'd want to go too,' people muttered among themselves.

Mrs Dan, our family friend who sheltered us when we were thrown out of our own home, had told us, in confidence:

'Our family is planning to escape, at any price. We can't live without freedom. We can't live under the Communists.'

Many of my friends had already *gone*. Now it was my turn.

Tin had been secretly organising the escape, with my parents' approval.

After delivering the bombshell, Tin asked my stepsister My, my older sister Ba and me to check if we had borrowed anything from anyone. These needed to be returned to the owners that day. 'In case they come and ask, and find out that no one's around,' he cautioned. Early the following morning we sneaked out of our apartment, each carrying nothing but a small bag containing a few pieces of clothing and some personal items. These were all we had to prepare us for the most momentous journey of our lives.

Tin gave each of us a fake travel permit to travel to Rach Gia, a province in the deep south of the Mekong Delta, the meeting point of our group of escapees. Rach Gia is two hundred kilometres south-west of Saigon. There were twenty-eight people in our group.

The organiser of our escape was Mrs Chung. Her husband, a former officer in the South Vietnamese army, was in a Communist prison. She planned the escape for their only daughter's future. My brother Tin was introduced to Mrs Chung through a friend.

She cut to the chase:

'Eight gold taels per person. However if you can find enough people, we are looking at three gold taels each. That's pretty cheap. I know all the contacts. We can depart in no time.'

Mrs Chung enlisted Tran, a former pilot in the South Vietnamese Air Force, to be the captain of our boat. For his service, his wife and his three young children would each have a place in the boat for free. Tran had managed to avoid the re-education camps by relocating his family to an isolated area in Rach Gia and assuming a new identity as a fisherman. We all fervently hoped that his skill in flying aircraft would help us cross the ocean.

Tam, a fisherman and another of Mrs Chung's contacts, was our steersman. He got the same deal as Tran. His wife and their infant daughter would travel for free.

Mrs Chung, Tran, and my resourceful brother Tin were joint commanders of this daring venture. They spent months working with each other on every aspect of the escape plan and oversaw the building of the boat from scratch. They did the test run in the river to make sure the boat was mechanically sound, then spent months scraping together enough fuel for the journey.

The wooden boat was 11 metres long and 1.6 metres wide. Over 5 metres of its length accommodated the bow, the stern and the cabin. With Tam at the steering wheel and Tran envisaging that he would sit on the boat roof for most of the trip to give direction — he had bought a school compass for this — the remaining twenty six people in the group would have to squeeze into a small cavity that was barely 6 metres long and 1.5 metres wide.

My group of escapees split into pairs, each boarding a separate bus to go to different safe houses in Rach Gia. I travelled with my stepsister My. For two weeks we lived the precarious lives of fugitives, moving from one safe house to another. One night Tam came to fetch us from our last shelter, a hut in the middle of nowhere, and brought us to our departure point in a riverboat.

The escape boat was moored in a secluded place in a mangrove swamp. Under the protection of a dense canopy that blocked the moonlight, we left the riverboat and stumbled our way through slushy ankle-deep mud to reach the escape boat.

It was slightly bigger than an average riverboat and nothing like the imposing and sturdy sea vessels that I had seen in picture books or in the movies. I remember thinking to myself, it's so tiny. Can we really cross the sea in this? The unsettling thought disappeared from my mind very quickly; I had no chance to dwell on it. The moment I stepped onto the boat was the moment of no return. This was my first step into the whirlwind of an out-of-this-world experience, a heart-stopping adventure, a complete and final departure from the life I had known before. Like a leaf tossed into a torrent, a powerful invisible force had hold of me and was pushing me towards wherever it wanted to take me.

As My and I squeezed ourselves on to the packed deck of the escape boat, wary faces were staring back at us out of the gloom. There were Tin, Ba, my little sister Linh, my stepbrother Tuan, my brother Chau, with his wife and their young daughter. The rest were close friends of my brother's and sister's, a close-knit group of former students of the French Lycee in Dalat.

It must have been very late that night or the early hours of the following morning when Mrs Chung did a final head-count. The little children had been put to sleep with pills. The hurricane lantern was put out, the anchor pulled up. Our steersman moved the boat slowly out of our hiding place with an oar. The gentle moonlight suddenly seemed too bright for the furtive travellers. Tam started the boat's engine. It let out a terrifying roar as it propelled the boat forward towards the open sea.

Day 1

For a long while we sat in silence, the gravity of the occasion etched on every face.

To escape from our country! To leave behind everything that was dear and familiar to us. To think of all the pain and the hopelessness that had driven us to desperation - and the only way out was this.

We were overwhelmed by our actions and weighed down by mixed emotions of fear and sadness, but our powerful dreams of freedom would eventually override these unsettling feelings and bring us back to our jolly mood. Like rainbow chasers, our hearts were filled with determination and hope. We might have to – literally – cross the sea and climb mountains to reach that elusive goal, but we had no doubt that we would. Absent from our thoughts was the fact that, from this moment on, we would be entirely at the mercy of fate.

The weather had been kind to us. The sea was calm. There was no wind. The morning sun revealed a flat and blue surface that seemed to spread forever into the far distance. This was my very first time at sea. I was surprised at how well I had been coping with seafaring.

I remembered the fun rides on colourful water bikes on Spring Fragrance Lake in Dalat, my hometown, and the trips in river boats and ferries during my stay in Rach Gia. Always there was the secure feeling that the shore was just a coo-ee away and destinations were measurable in time and distance.

The sea was much bigger than all those rivers combined, but I wasn't at all scared. The meanest character associated with the sea that I had ever known was Captain Hook in the Peter Pan children's series. I had read Ernest Hemingway's *The old man and the sea*. I had watched movies where lovers parted and blew kisses in the wind as the ship let out a sonorous hoot. The sea, to me, embodied romance and adventure.

Our boat was not much bigger than an average riverboat— we sat crammed tight in two rows facing each other—and yet I no longer felt afraid. That notion of romance and adventure kept my spirit up and cast aside all sense of foreboding.

Day 2

In the afternoon, the sea turned restless. Our boat started to rock strongly from side to side. Seasickness arrived with a vengeance.

I lay helplessly on the boat floor. My stomach churned up and down with the undulation of the relentless waves. My legs, stretched out and lifeless, weighed heavily on the shoulders of those sitting opposite me, while theirs lay on mine.

From the boat roof Tran, the skipper, yelled out:

'There's a huge cloud build-up. A storm is coming!'

His voice was full of panic.

The sky turned grey; the faint sun disappeared. The wind was howling while the waves kept rising. The rain, trickling at first, rapidly turned into a downpour. It was too dangerous to plough over these water hills; vats of it had splashed into the boat, now a battered piece of wood shoved in all directions, struggling to stay afloat.

'Stop the engine!' Tran shouted.

'Scoop the water out!' my brother Tin screamed. 'Whoever can stand up, splash the water out!'

Suddenly the waves swelled to three metres high, knocking the boat off balance and about to thrust it down into the raging sea.

'Everyone! Move to the left!'

Tran, lying on his stomach and clinging to the boat roof, let out his desperate cries. In the wind they sounded like echoes from far away.

'Move to the right!'

'Left!'

'Right!'

'Left!'

'Right!'

People hastily threw their bodies on top of each other from this side of the boat to the other side, then from that side to this side, again and again, to help maintain its precarious balance. I saw the dark sky going up and down and the frightened faces of my companions. Cold sea water splashed all over my body. I smelled vomit. I heard heartfelt prayers.

With my eyes tightly shut, I pleaded to Quan Yin, the female Buddha of Compassion:

'Quan Yin, please save me! Quan Yin, please save me!'

How many times I called on her, I did not know. Strangely, I felt a sense of comfort within. The prayers helped my mind focus and blocked out my fear.

After what seemed like a very long time, the storm subsided, then blew away.

We looked at each other. Everyone's hair was drenched in a mixture of sea water and engine oil. Our clothes, clinging wet to our bodies, smelled of engine oil, urine and vomit. They would dry very soon, caked in these substances, stiff like cardboard, as the bright sun came. We were badly dishevelled, but alive.

There was cause to smile again.

The woven bamboo matting on the roof of our boat was in tatters, but the boat itself was still structurally sound. A thick layer of long, hollow bamboo stems fastened together and strapped to two sides of the boat, a primitive floatation device, had helped keep it afloat.

But the big waves were returning.

Tran did not want to take any chances.

'There's an island in front of us! We'd better take a rest! It's too risky to press on!' he yelled from the boat roof.

He had been sitting on it since our departure two days before, giving direction to the steering crew below with the help of the school compass.

'Are we approaching international waters yet?' Mrs Chung asked.

She sat at the bow, now and then giving assurance to the group of youngsters under her charge.

'Not yet, but we will very soon,' Tran said. He chuckled. 'Our grandpas from the Communist security police may still be snoring right now in their beds! Can you believe it! Not one patrol boat in sight!'

'How are you doing up there, Tran?' someone asked.

'Hey, man, make sure you sit very still up there and don't fall down, OK?'

The obvious caution made everyone laugh.

Like Robinson Crusoe, twenty-eight of us set foot on the pristine sand, tentatively making our way onto the deserted island.

The afternoon sun shed its gentle light over the lush forest. Birds singing and the shuffling of leaves in the soft breeze seemed to be the island's only disturbances. Tam, the steersman, went for a quick check around the island and soon came back. This tiny islet was just a short walk from one end to the other, he said. A sparkling stream of water from a small rivulet wove its way through clumps of wild plants. I dipped my face into the stream, scooped the water with both hands and had a good drink. The water tasted so sweet and the air was so fresh.

There was a small hut at the top of a small hill. Tam told everyone to wait in the forest while he climbed the hill. When he got there, he went inside for a quick check, then came out and yelled down:

'It's OK! There's no one around! You can come up!'

The hut appeared abandoned. There was no sign of anyone currently living in it, except for a small pile of cold ashes from a long extinguished fire in the middle of the dirt floor and a few pieces of sticks scattered around.

'Someone has been here.' Mrs Chung was anxious.

'There's nothing to worry about,' Tam assured her. 'This is a storm shelter for fishermen. I've seen similar huts on other islands.'

Tam was a local fisherman. His assurance put everyone at ease.

We set up a fire and cooked some rice soup. After the light meal, Mrs Chung urged everyone to have a rest on the beach in preparation for the long journey ahead.

I lay on the bare sand. It was still warm from the heat of the day. I could not fall asleep right away. My mind was reliving the excitement of my first day at sea. The air was getting cooler as the sun was about to set. Mosquitoes started coming out in droves. I figured they must be thrilled at having the rare chance to taste the sweet blood of city folks and determined to make the most of the occasion. I moved my hands up and down over my body repeatedly in the vain hope of driving them away, but got tired and gave up. They had their feed then left me alone. My body was maddeningly itchy, but experience told me if I started scratching, I would feel itchier and would never stop. I gritted my teeth and, with superhuman resolve, only rubbed my hands gently on the bites whenever I felt I could not take it anymore. The sand started to lose its warmth. The itchiness subsided. The cool breeze coming in from the beach gave me goosebumps. Darkness fell. Millions of stars were twinkling in the sky. As I listened to the murmur of the sea, I thought to myself this landscape was as beautiful as poetry, and drifted off to sleep with that happy thought.

Day 3

We woke up to a beautiful morning. The boys paddled out to the boat and brought in a few loaves of rice cakes wrapped in banana leaves. This was our third day on the run. We had to be very careful with our food supply. We savoured our ration of one slice of cake each, then flocked to the stream to have a good drink.

The clear sky, the blue sea and the tweeting of the birds in the trees had calmed my nerves somewhat. The sight of pretty wild flowers scattered along the bank of the rivulet gave me a happy feeling. Everything was so pleasant and beautiful. I momentarily forgot that in the eye of the Communist authorities, we were fleeing criminals. We shouldn't be having such a good time as this.

Our joint commanders decided to continue the journey late in the afternoon.

While the steering crew gave the boat a maintenance check-up, a few boys carried the drinking water containers to the stream for refill. The rest of the group went further inland to explore.

This island was a coconut forest. The sight of tall coconut trees crowded with bunches of voluptuous fruit dangling in the breeze brought a loud cheer from everyone. The fruits were so ripe that some of them would just drop to the ground. Now and then we would hear a nice thump and there it was, still rolling on the ground, a green and plump coconut bursting with juice.

Sam, Tin's friend, climbed up the coconut trees like a monkey. With a light shake of the hand, he removed each fruit one by one from its stalk, then leisurely threw it to the ground.

We spent the day sitting on stone slabs under the shade of the trees, relishing the soft flesh and the thirst-quenching juice of the coconuts, chatting and laughing as though there was not a thing to worry about in the world.

Suddenly the boys who had been working on the boat ran in from the beach and alerted everyone:

'Scatter yourselves! Hide somewhere! Someone's coming!'

The cheerful mood immediately turned to fright.

Everyone sprinted away in different directions. I did not know how far or how long I had run, the only thought that occupied my mind was to get behind a bush deep in the island. I managed to reach suitable cover just when my legs were about to give way. I slumped behind it, trembling uncontrollably. My chest was heaving with every breath. My heart was pounding so loudly it almost drowned out the sound of the approaching boat. I was pretty sure that from the distance of the beach, the person, or persons, on that boat could not see me, but I still wrapped my arms tight around my huddled body, perhaps a natural reflex to make myself small and as invisible as possible, in order to protect myself from danger. Then there was silence. The engine of the approaching boat had been turned off.

For a long while I sat like a frozen statue in my hiding place. It was getting dark. I could hear loud talking coming out of the hut. Then the sound of footsteps and Tam's familiar voice calling:

'Hey, everybody! Where are you hiding? You can come out now.'

Emerging from our hiding places, we followed Tam to the hut where an extraordinary scene was unfolding.

A man was sitting on the earth floor with his hands tied behind his back, his face pale with fear. Sam was pacing back and forth, now and then waving a gun at the stranger's face.

'You've come here alone or you're with someone else?' Sam was shouting and fuming. 'What's your plan? Following us like this?'

'N...o... It's j...ust m...e...,' the man quivered.

'You are from the security police? Aren't you?'

'N...o... I'm n...ot... I saw your boat... I was curious... I just came to the island to see what's going on. Please spare me.'

'I've been to prison and I don't fucking give a damn about the security police! You understand? You are not to lie to me, you understand?'

Sam made a threatening movement with the gun, casting a frightening shadow on the mud wall of the hut. A small fire had been lit. It was no longer light outside.

'Please spare me. Please let me go back to my family,' the man pleaded.

His voice was waning; he realised the hopeless situation he found himself in. Through the flickering flame, the silent crowd encircling him resembled menacing ghosts, or worse, desperate fugitives who could resort to desperate action.

Mrs Chung, Tran and Tin went outside to discuss strategy. It was too risky to let the man go. He could raise the alarm. He could bring back reinforcements. He could foil the escape.

Tin ordered everyone to run to the beach and get into our boat. The man was escorted back onto his boat, which was tied to ours. We departed from the island, towing the man's boat for a long enough distance to prevent him from getting back to the mainland too soon, then set it free.

The man had tried to blackmail us. When he stepped on the island, he had encountered Mrs Chung and Tin. They clearly didn't look like local peasants. This aroused his immediate suspicion.

'I know what you people are up to,' he had said.

He had threatened to sail back to alert the security police if they did not give him money. While Mrs Chung tried to stall him, Tin signaled to the boys nearby to come out of their hiding places. He enlisted Sam to play the bad guy, to give the man a bit of a fright. The man crumbled when he realised there were so many of us. Before putting him back on his boat, we emptied all the coins and notes in our pockets and gave them to him. We would be sailing to a far, far away place, the

Vietnamese *dong* would be of no use to us. Our extortionist could not believe his change of fortune.

Sam's convincing performance earned him a big rave from all of us. He always stood out in school plays.

He had finished high school but failed to get into university because of his 'tainted' background. His father, a former officer of the vanquished South Vietnamese government, was locked up in a Communist prison.

That night, we boys and girls had a fun time mimicking Sam's 'rough man' manner.

'Look, I pretended to be rough and tough, but the truth was, deep down, I was as scared as hell!' Sam admitted. 'Good God! That was the first time I ever held a gun in my hand! Didn't you see my hand tremble while I was holding it?'

The sound of our cheerful laughter was heard from a most unlikely place - a lonely boat on the high seas.

The boat surged forward, carrying with it our hopes and dreams.

Day 4

We traveled south-westward, aiming for Thailand or Malaysia. At some time in the morning, Tran yelled down from the boat roof:

'We have entered international waters!'

Everyone broke into a loud cheer.

The sea was in a good mood; its colour was a magnificent emerald blue that seemed to stretch forever towards a mystical realm beyond anyone's reach.

'Long live freedom!' Sam yelled.

A chain of joyful praise to freedom followed, in all the languages that we could think of.

In Vietnamese:
'Tu do muon nam!'
In French:
'Vive la liberte!'
In Italian:

'Viva la liberta!'

Our French education did have some use.

'When we reach the shore of freedom, there will be Western journalists waiting to welcome us. They will be totally bowled over by the fact that it was a woman - a Vietnamese woman - who led this escape feat. They will be amazed at such a heroic act. Daring to cross the sea for freedom!' Mrs Chung's voice was full of pride.

Our celebration would prove to be premature. The shore of freedom was still a long way away.

The boat continued its lonely sail across international waters. There was no land in sight and no other boats on the horizon. There seemed to be no other sound except for the quiet, powerful thrust of the undersea currents. We had no radio equipment nor life-saving devices. Another bout of rough weather and we might all be tossed into the sea and disappear without any trace, but having reached international waters, feeling ebullient that we were now out of the grip of the Communists, it seemed no one was thinking of such a possibility. Perhaps the older ones were, but they wisely kept it to themselves so as not to affect the kids' morale. The youngsters continued to carry on like a bunch of bubbly students on an excursion of a lifetime. Well, we *were* a bunch of students on *the* excursion of a lifetime.

'Who prayed the loudest during the storm?'

'I looked at Sam and his face was as green as a leaf.'

'How could you see anything? I saw you pray with your eyes shut!'

'You know, I have made a solemn promise to Buddha. If we reach the shore safely, I will go vegetarian for a good three months!'

For a while, a family of porpoises delighted us with their company, gliding effortlessly along our boat. I felt as though I could just reach my hand into the water and pat them on their glistening skin.

'Porpoises are human's friends,' Mrs Chung said. Her serious voice reflected her respect for these delightful creatures. 'If you see them, you are very lucky. They save you in times of trouble. They are the guardian angels of the sea. They swim along the boat to protect you, to keep your boat from capsizing.'

But there were sharks in the ocean too, and no one wanted to think of that.

We had run out of food. The plastic drinking water containers were passed around; each person was allowed one last drink.

Luckily we did not have to face hunger and thirst this soon.

'There's an island ahead!' Tam yelled from the boat roof. He had swapped place with Tran.

I craned my neck to look. In the far distance, a green patch, perhaps the canopy of a palm forest, slowly emerged from the permanent blue horizontal line that separated the sky and the sea.

Tran navigated the boat close to the island then dropped the anchor. Its inhabitants, as exotic as a people from a far away tropical island can be, lined themselves along the beach of this tiny island to watch us approach. The men, women and children all wore colourful sarongs. Their brown skin was smooth and shiny; the women had white horizontal stripes painted across their cheeks. They could have just jumped out from the pages of National Geographic.

Tam and another boy paddled in to ask for drinking water.

From our boat I could see the tallest and most imposing man of the tribe, possibly their chief, make frenzied hand gestures to Tam. He flapped his arms up and down, and kept pointing at the direction we were heading, then at Tam's wrist. He seemed frustrated by the language barrier which prevented him from conveying something important to us.

Tam and the boy came back with the drink containers replenished.

As we waved these islanders goodbye, I could still see the tribal chief jumping up and down in frustration on the sandy beach.

'What did the elderly man want to say?' I wondered out loud.

'I think he warned me to be careful; someone might want to strip my watch,' Tam said matter-of-factly. He did not appear to be concerned about this, or perhaps he did, but decided to keep it to himself because he did not want to unnerve us.

After four lonely days at sea, the sight of land and our recent contact with another group of human beings had lifted our spirits. Our encounter with these exotic islanders meant that we had entered another country's territory. We had truly left Vietnam behind. From now on it would be just a matter of finding a safe haven. It was going to be much harder than anyone could foresee.

On the map of Southeast Asia, there is a small blue patch that links Vietnam's southwest coast with Thailand's and Malaysia's east coast. In real life, this small blue patch covers approximately three hundred nautical miles and harbours untold dangers. We were crossing it.

We spotted a fishing boat painted in a peculiar, colourful pattern. Sam tried to catch its attention by standing at the bow waving his white T-shirt – an exact rendition of a classic stranded-at-sea movie scene. The colourful boat parked next to ours. A peasant couple who stood at the wheel looked out.

Sam rubbed his tummy, shook his head, pointing to the children in our boat.

The couple's faces were full of compassion. The man lowered a bucket of cooked rice to us with a rope. Another bucket of sugar water with ice cubes floating refreshingly in it followed. We waved them good-bye with the biggest smiles of appreciation on our faces.

We ate the fluffy cooked rice off our hands, drank the ice-cold sugar water straight from the bucket and munched the crunchy ice cubes. This was luxurious! It was not just because we had been without food and drink for a whole day. It was also because for three years since the Communist victory, South Vietnamese had subsisted mainly on a diet of sweet potatoes and Job's tears – the hard seeds grown from wild grass normally fed to horses. We hardly saw any white rice or sugar in our food ration. Yet this Thai peasant couple could afford to give all this to us so generously.

This told me that Thailand had become more prosperous, while Vietnam was left behind, sinking deeper and deeper into unprecedented poverty.

There were more sightings of other boats. We had arrived at something like a water highway.

I could see the black hull of a big ship on the faraway horizon. It travelled in our direction. Our hopes swelled. This ship could rescue us! It could allow us to board and bring us to a free country!

Sam waved the white flag frantically.

We had been exposed to the sun for four days now. We had been wearing the same outfits, now weatherworn and caked in a mixture of engine oil, vomit, urine, sweat and sea water. We looked dark and filthy.

The imposing ship, seemingly preoccupied with its own importance, continued its course unperturbed. We were not worthy of its attention.

'Bastards!' Sam swore.

A few boats hurried past. Seafaring at this fair distance from the mainland seemed to be only for those with a business to attend to and no time to waste. A couple of small boats stopped by, giving us food and water. That was how we survived.

That night we were treated to a spectacular light show. From afar, the dazzling lights of a big seaport brought the dark sky to life, renewing our hope to be able to land.

As our boat came near the rocky cliff towards the port entrance, it got stuck in a bed of rocks. The boys immediately jumped into the water, half-immersing themselves to heave it out to the clear, and push it to the harbour.

I felt a surge of admiration for the boys. They had been doing all the hard work on this trip while we girls just sat in the boat doing nothing, like a bunch of useless princesses.

This immense port was crowded with numerous ships and boats of different heights and sizes moored alongside each other. Under a star-studded sky, the bright streams of light emitted from these ships and boats and the giant electricity poles on top of the cliffs gave this place a warm and glamorous feel.

Those who stayed on these vessels must be having their night rests, I thought. There was no one around to notice a group of Vietnamese riff-raff had just sneaked into the harbour. Like a beggar in a busy market, we stood out like an eyesore in this beautiful place, yet managed to be invisible and insignificant at the same time.

We parked our boat near the bottom of a brightly-lit three-decker cruise liner. We were hungry and desperate for someone's attention.

A man in a white chef hat darted in and out of the liner's lower deck. He looked like a cook in the middle of cleaning tasks. He was about to tip a bucket into the sea when he caught sight of us frantically waving and calling up to him. Sam made the tummy rubbing movement and pleaded loudly. 'Help! Food please!'

The cook went into the cabin, then reappeared on the deck with another man. With a rope, the two men lowered down a bucket of food to us, retrieved the rope, then disappeared.

'Let's see what yummy things these people gave us!' I waited excitedly for my turn to eat.

It was a big disappointment. The cooked rice, mixed with an indefinable brownish sauce, tasted like it was about to go stale. It might be something the cook was about to throw into the sea! I cringed as I shoved a handful of rice down my throat, just to have something in my stomach to appease my hunger.

The harbour seemed to be a safe place to pass the night. We had been sitting in one position, crammed next to each other throughout the journey. There was not much difference, whether we were awake or asleep, except that when sleeping, we rested our heads on our knees. I was about to doze off when I heard Tran's panicky cry from the boat roof:

'What! What's going on here! You people down there! Wake up! What do these bastards want?'

Everyone was shaken out of their hazy dreams. Out of nowhere, two men hopped onto our boat. They strode along its length forcefully, stepped over people's knees and feet, making our boat rock from side to side. In the dark, I could not see their faces clearly, but I remember their hawk-like stares.

They had positioned their big boat close to ours. The men in the big boat threw the intruders a rope. They tied it to our boat frame, then climbed on a ladder to get back to their boat. The big boat started to move, pulling ours along.

'Songkla! Songkla!' the intruders and their gang yelled out excitedly, incomprehensibly.

'Chop the rope off! Cut it!' Tran screamed to the boys below. 'Chop it! Right now!' Tran cried in panic.

The rope was finally severed with a machete.

It was only much later that I understood the chilling significance of this incident. Songkla is Thailand's seaport and also a notorious pirate stronghold. Thousands of Boat People got towed to Songkla by pirate ships, thinking they were being helped to reach the shore. They would be robbed, the women and the girls would be raped or kidnapped. Many did not survive to tell their tales.

Day 5
Having survived the kidnap attempt, everyone felt shaken. We waited impatiently for the night to pass.

In the morning the quiet harbour sprang to life. Like a column of ants, wharfies appeared in droves, going about their tasks, loading and unloading thousands of crates to and from the towering ships with frenzied precision. In this systematic hurly-burly, where everyone seemed to know exactly where they fitted into the whole machinery, our tattered boat was clearly out of place.

Tran trotted up and down the busy quay trying in vain to get help. No one had the time or patience to stop for the man in rags whose haggard face had been blackened by oil engine fumes. He tried to communicate to passers-by by making incomprehensible hand gestures and ended up looking like a deranged person.

We left the harbour and aimed south, towards Malaysia. The sea traffic was getting busier. We no longer felt lonely. Hopefully a passing boat would stop and someone could point us in the right direction so we could land.

Our sense of reassurance would soon be shattered. We did not know that the vast sea that stretched to infinity still remained as it was in primordial time, an aquatic wilderness. We were unprepared for the attacks of the savages.

A boat appeared on the horizon. With other boats, we had to wave our white flag for their attention. This one headed straight towards us.

'My God! The pirates! The pirates!' Tran's hair-raising scream from the boat roof sent a chill down my bones.

The loud and powerful noise of the pirate boat engine broke the silence of the sea. Our boat lurched from side to side as the pirate boat swerved wildly around it before ramming it to a stop.

Through the gap between the gunwale and the boat roof, I saw a dark-skinned man with a colourful bandanna tied around his head. The sharp blade of his machete gleamed between his clenched teeth.

I was paralysed with fear.

Two pirates jumped onto our boat and searched everyone. Sam quickly threw his gun into the water. The men and the boys raised their arms in the air in submission; the women and the girls cupped their hands in front of their chests and bowed repeatedly to the pirates, pleading for mercy.

A pirate's face was right opposite mine, I could feel his foul and heavy breathing. He put his hand inside my underpants to search for valuables, then moved to the next person.

The pirates took all our bags and any valuables that they could see. Those who wore rings and watches, even prescribed glasses, were forced to remove them and hand them over.

The moment the robbers left, Tam started the boat again. There was not even time to breathe out a sigh of relief. We just had to move on.

At least our lives were spared.

The women and the girls cupped their hands together to say thanks to God and Buddha.

Oh God and Buddha, please show us the way to safety.

We had been at sea for five days now. Before this attack, the sight of another seafarer would give us a sense of comfort. We could ask them for food and water that would sustain us for another day. Our seemingly interminable spell of loneliness in the vast silent sea would be broken, temporarily at least.

Now we were stricken with apprehension. What could happen to us next?

Nature can be dangerous and unpredictable, but it is never as evil as human cruelty. The high sea is a lawless terrain and a perfect crime scene. No one hears your cry for help. The waves wash away all evidence. Only the sky and the sea bear silent witness.

Soon enough, another boat appeared.

It headed straight towards us and powered dangerously alongside our boat, forcing us to stop. We all knew the pirates routine by now.

Two men jumped onto our boat. They quickly walked from bow to stern, making a quick assessment of each and every one of us with their cold stares. Tam gestured to them and made stripping movements over his fingers and wrists to let them know that we had already been robbed and now had nothing of value.

It suddenly occurred to me that our current predicament was the very thing of which the tribal chief from the exotic island had tried to warn us. 'Don't go this way! The pirates will attack you and rob you!' Yes, this was what he had tried to say to us with his frantic gestures. Unfortunately we had not understood him. Even if we had, and had taken his warnings seriously, I doubted that would have changed anything. To turn the boat around? To head back to Vietnam, the Communist hell that we had fled from? That was an impossibility.

The pirates realised they had picked the wrong victims. They left empty-handed, but just as suddenly, they came back. As if they'd had second thoughts.

What happened next may have been so traumatic that it has been purged from my memory. I remember finding myself standing on the pirate boat with Van, my sister Ba's friend, but I don't recall how I got there.

Was I forced to jump onto the pirate boat? Did the pirates drag me on board and, stricken with fear, I didn't dare resist? Did anyone from our boat try to prevent this from happening? Or was this turn of events so shocking that everyone was caught by surprise and, for a critical moment, did not know what to do? I just don't know.

Luckily for me and Van, our male boat companions, including my brothers and my stepbrother, quickly recovered from the initial shock. They jumped straight onto the pirate boat after us. Their faces went pale with anger, or fear, or both. Taking an aggressive stand, raising their fists, they stared coldly at the criminals, giving them a clear sign that they were prepared to fight to the end.

As brazen as they were, this pirate gang comprised only three rough-looking men. One was busy minding the wheel. They were outnumbered.

After a momentary standoff, they quietly stood aside to let us return to our boat.

Van broke down and cried.

I do not recall feeling particularly distressed at the time, perhaps because what happened was too far removed from anything I had experienced before. My brain had not quite managed to grasp it and make any sense out of it. I felt like a spectator of a horror movie, watching something terrible happen to someone else and not to me. Psychiatrists call this mental state, often experienced by trauma victims, dissociation.

Yet more than three decades later this nightmarish scene still comes back to haunt me again and again. I wake up in the middle of the night, sweating, shuddering, terrified. I struggle to go back to sleep. I just lie in bed, staring at the dark, thinking about what could have happened to me, to my female companions, and all the horror that entailed.

Having foiled the kidnap attempt, everyone was in a sombre mood.

The calm sea no longer brought comfort. Would there be another pirate attack? I was sure this was on everyone's mind.

We gauged the time of day by observing the position of the sun. It had been a while since I felt its burning rays over the top of my head.

The children slumped on their mothers' laps. The adults tried hard to maintain their spirits.

Since leaving the big port at dawn, besides the encounters with the pirates, we did not see any other boats.

Perhaps the seasoned seafarers knew this was a notorious area and wisely avoided it. Only inexperienced and desperate people like us would unsuspectingly head into these dangerous waters.

We pricked up our ears at the revving sound of a boat engine and made our tentative way towards it. Would this boat turn out to be another pirate boat? We could not know for sure. But we were all hungry and thirsty, especially the children. We had no choice.

A two-decker trawler appeared in front of our eyes. It moved slowly before coming to a stop. Its heavy crane gradually emerged from under thick spouts of water.

A dozen tall and dark men, bare-chested and muscular, each wearing just a calf-length sarong tied around their waists, flocked from their cabin onto the deck, readying themselves to haul in their catch. This was a Thai fishing crew.

Unlike the pirates who ferociously lunged their boats towards us, these people seemed engrossed in their tasks and were not paying us much attention. We felt somewhat assured.

A man of Chinese appearance popped his head out from the glass window of the trawler's upper cabin. Tam waved at him and talked to him in Chinese. Tam was a Vietnamese of Chinese descent. The man answered back.

'Lucky! This man speaks Cantonese!' Tam exclaimed. He seemed clearly relieved.

The Chinese seemed to be the boss of this fishing crew. He allowed us to board and gave us iced water to drink. The women and the girls were ushered into the air-conditioned cabin, while the men and the boys stood outside on the deck.

Compared with our boat's crammed and dirty condition, the trawler's spacious cabin with its smooth polished floorboard was as stylish as a five-star hotel. It had a low ceiling designed not for standing up, but for the crew to sit or to lie down to rest. I felt so relieved that I could stretch my legs.

Outside, the crane had fully emerged from the water and was being hoisted up in the air. In its jaws dangled a giant net bursting with all kinds of fish and sea creatures. The crane slowly swung the net inwards, right over the surface of the deck, then relaxed its jaws. A mountain of fish spewed out and soon lay writhing on the platform. The men quickly shoveled them into huge ice containers, then carried them down to the below-deck cold compartment.

In a short time, all the fish had been cleared. The men swayed their sarong-clad bodies, clapped their hands and tapped their feet to a strange singing tune, in what seemed like a dance ritual to celebrate an abundant catch. They resembled the Egyptian slaves who built the pyramids, or the hunters and gatherers of prehistoric time - men in their primal state.

After the dance, they cleaned the floor and washed themselves with a hose.

Their work was done. The sun was about to set. They retreated into the cabin and sat among the women and girls. Our men and boys were also allowed into the cabin.

In the kitchen corner, the cook had been toiling with his pots and pans the whole time. I was looking forward to a feast of fresh fish. The wonderful smell from the kitchen filled up my lungs. I felt better already.

Suddenly Ban, my brother Tin's friend, approached me hastily and talked in a low voice, an alarmed look on his face:

'Quynh, if any of these men comes close to you, point at me and do this.' He placed his two index fingers close and in parallel with each other. 'This tells them that you and I are husband and wife, we are a pair. Remember to do that, OK?'

I gave him a puzzled look. I wondered to myself why he looked so tense, so worried, when everything seemed to be alright; the cook was about to bring out the food and we were about to have a good meal.

Tin and Sam went around to tell other girls what Ban had just told me. We girls and boys were now all paired up as married couples. I was too naive to understand the reason we had to do this and totally unaware of the horrific scenario that must have been running through the boys' minds. I just found this pairing quite amusing.

The cook passed huge bowls of cooked rice and plates of fresh fish, steamed or stir-fried with vegetables, to be placed on the cabin floorboards. Together with the fishing crew, we sat in small circles relishing the wholesome meal. The boat owner invited Tam and his two-year-old daughter to the upper cabin to have dinner with him.

It was dark outside. The sea had gone to sleep. Inside the trawler, under a warm amber light, a group of strangers shared pots of hot tea with each other.

The atmosphere was so congenial, Tran thought up a fun idea.

'Well, these guys are really nice to us. How about we treat them with some light entertainment?'

We clapped hands and sang all the sing-a-long songs that we could remember. To the fishermen's delight, Tran's children stood up and sang. Inspired, a couple of them also sang some Thai songs.

The Chinese boss, Tam and his daughter came down from the upper cabin to join the audience of this spontaneous cabaret show.

'I don't know why, but the boat owner really takes to my daughter; he wants to adopt her,' Tam smiled in delight.

His daughter was as cute as a china doll.

That night the dozen men of the fishing crew and twenty-eight of us slept on the cabin floor next to each other like sardines.

The men in our group might lie down with their eyes only half-closed, but I nodded off almost immediately, blissful in my ignorance.

The following morning my heart sank as we had to leave the comfort of the trawler and go back to our rickety boat. The Chinese man explained that he could not tow us to the Thai shore. He would be in trouble with the Thai government if he did. He told us to aim south for Malaysia.

In our lonely journey at sea, cut off from the world, we did not know that Vietnamese Boat People were no longer welcome.

Thailand no longer allowed Boat People to land, while Malaysia had begun the 'push back' policy. Many refugee boats managed to reach the Malaysian shore, only to be pushed back to sea and left to their own fate.

Day 6

After a comfortable night in the trawler, we found ourselves alone again at the mercy of the treacherous sea. It was daunting. I felt scared.

How long would we have to stay adrift like this? How long before a big wave would come and toss us all into the sea? How long could we withstand this precarious existence?

The sea seemed impervious to the human drama that was unfolding. Dusk was falling and land was always out of sight. We were approaching the point of panic.

Suddenly, in the purple twilight, the black hull of a ship appeared. Everyone was hopeful and excited again. It could be the answer to our prayers.

Sam waved the white flag frantically.

I strained my eyes towards the dark horizon. Yes, I could see it! My heart beat happily, like someone who had just spotted an oasis in the desert.

Our guardian angel had arrived, in the shape of an imposing frigate from the Thai Navy. It moved slowly towards us, then stopped at a safe distance so as not to cause strong waves that could overwhelm our boat. Tam rushed our boat towards it, for fear that, like a mirage, it would disappear.

From the height of the gunwale of the towering ship, a rope ladder was thrown down.

We took turns to climb up the ladder. Once reaching the gunwale, each of us would be pulled in by the navy men.

The captain of the frigate, a man in his thirties in impeccable uniform, with a kindly face and a quietly authoritative manner, stood near the gunwale to oversee our rescue.

When my turn came, I bit my lips and gripped the rope with all the strength that I could muster. I tried hard to lift my feet up the ladder one wobbly step at a time. To reach the gunwale's lofty height seemed an impossible task for me. Since I was little, I had always been frail, timid and scared of heights. At school I showed absolutely no talent for sports and was always picked last in any team-based physical contest. Now I was doing rope climbing in the middle of the sea, sweating and trembling all the way, too frightened for my life to look down at the dark waters below.

I made it, finally. My survival instinct was strong enough to pull me through this incredible challenge.

Once we were all on board, the sailors led us to a large open deck at the stern. We were not allowed inside the control centre, for security reasons, of course. However we could stand outside the glass windows looking in. The interior of the frigate was immense. With all the sparkling panels, the modern equipment and millions of shiny buttons and flashing lights, it looked like the interior of a space shuttle.

The sailors, in their smart uniforms, gave us hot tea and biscuits, and milk for the toddlers. The hot drinks warmed our stomachs while the sailors' smiles warmed our hearts. Now and then the handsome captain came over to make sure that we were well looked after. It felt so good to be cared for.

When I was pulled into the ship, the back of my weatherworn shirt was torn, exposing my back. An officer quickly went away and came back with a beautiful and elaborately embroidered shirt, a traditional outfit often worn by Thai males. It could be from his own wardrobe, to be worn on shore leave. He gave it to me and I wore it over my torn shirt.

We expressed our gratitude to these gentlemen of the Thai navy by nodding our heads, smiling and saying 'thank you' profusely. We spent the warm night sitting up or lying down on the deck. A few sailors came in and out of their cabins throughout the night. When walking past us, they always had a nice and sympathetic smile on their faces. We had a friendly chat with some of them in broken English.

'We thank you! You very nice! We thank you!' Tran said.

'You very nice too!' a sailor returned the compliment.

'You know, Communists, no good. Vietnamese Communists, no good. Very bad! Very bad!' Ban tried to explain our plight to him. 'Killing... prison... everything!'

'I know. Vietnamese Communists, no good,' the sailor nodded.

'Thai people! Very nice! Very good! We thank you! Thank you! You very nice!'

'Vietnamese people very nice too! I love Vietnamese people! I love Vietnamese people!'

The reality of human politics would soon interfere and spoil this precious moment of human love. Like the fishing crew that rescued us before, these sailors could give us overnight shelter but could not lead us to the Thai shore. Allowing us to board, the captain may have already defied orders.

The following morning we had to go back to our boat.

The captain and his crew were clearly distressed at having to make this heartbreaking decision. They all looked sombre, as though dark clouds had descended and hung heavily on their conscience.

The captain showed our skipper the direction to Malaysia. We exchanged our sad farewells. The young sailor who'd had a chat with us the night before could not contain his tears.

My heart was heavy. If I were to survive, I thought to myself, the Thai shirt I was wearing would be a special reminder of this moving encounter.

The frigate maintained its reassuring presence on the horizon to see us cross safely into Malaysian waters. The night before, perhaps against international maritime rules, it had moved closer to the Malaysian border to facilitate our journey.

Now and then we turned our heads towards the direction of our rescuers, smiling, waving. We were sure our guardian angels were watching us from afar with their binoculars. We kept turning around, smiling and waving as the frigate became smaller and smaller and finally disappeared behind the flat blue line.

Day 7

The soothing breeze and the fresh morning air had restored our spirits.

Our boat entered a canal that branched into numerous waterways. We took a narrow stream that wove past half-immersed tropical plants, tall dead trees and overhanging branches. Nothing prepared us for the magnificent opening at the end of this water labyrinth.

An immense lake appeared in front of our eyes. It was surrounded by beautiful villas painted in a variety of bright and delightful colours: canary yellow, burgundy, white, lime green or aqua blue.

A family was preparing for an early picnic by the lake. The father was spreading a rug on the green grass, the mother was sorting things out from a picnic basket and their children were running around playfully. When they spotted us, we waved and smiled happily at them. The mother and the children smiled back, but the father was hesitant. It was clear he had no idea what to do with a bunch of people in rags who suddenly appeared from nowhere. We were as relevant to this place as a stain on a beautiful masterpiece.

After all the traumas at sea, this peaceful scene of normal living struck me as extraordinary. I looked at it longingly, as though it could only happen in my wishful thinking. It felt like a long time since I last saw a family having a picnic by a lake. It seemed quite remote from our current predicament, drifting from place to place like flotsam and jetsam, desperate for a safe haven. 'These people are so blessed!' I exclaimed enviously to myself.

We tied our boat to a small footbridge and quietly waited for someone to come to our assistance.

From a villa opposite, at a short distance from the footbridge, a tall and distinguished man in starched white ceremonial army uniform with golden stars on his epaulettes came out and strode towards us. His grand entrance into this already magnificent setting – the blue lake, the beautiful sky and the exquisite villas - was like a scene from a movie. He had the bearing of someone very important, most likely a general. There were a couple of flashy cars parked in front of his villa. A couple of assistants, also in army uniform, fussed after him.

Like a God, the general stood on the footbridge looking down on us as we, from our tattered boat moored under the bridge, looked up to him reverentially, pleading for a miracle.

'We… from Vietnam. SOS! Please help!' Sam said, holding the white flag.

The general's face was full of concern.

By now more and more people had come out from their villas. They stood on the bank of the lake watching us as we were watching them, in mutual intrigue and curiosity. The men and the women had dark, smooth skin and wore beautiful colourful sarongs. The women covered their heads with embroidered silk shawls; they seemed weighed down by the amount of gold bracelets and gold earrings they had on them. We—sea-battered and harrowed-looking—we were a pitiful spectacle ourselves.

The general and his assistants walked to their cars and drove away.

A short while later, two policemen and a female nurse arrived in two jeeps, most likely at the general's request. The policemen helped lift the women and the children onto the bridge. The nurse gave each of us two jabs on the arm against smallpox and cholera.

After seven days at sea, it was nice to feel the firm land under one's feet again. It seemed to bob up and down, up and down, like ocean waves. I sat down to touch the ground and grip the grass with both hands, to reassure myself that the waves would not come and sweep me back to sea again. It would take me a while to be rid of that sensation.

Our little boat, aptly named 'Freedom', had finally brought us to freedom.

It had been a friend to us; it had been a part of us; it had braved the wind and the storm to deliver us to safety. It was the unsung hero in this eventful journey.

Yet looking at it from the bank of the lake, I was startled to see how fragile, how tiny it was. How on earth could we cross the sea in that flimsy piece of wood!

Besides a miracle, how else could I explain our survival?

PART II
KOTA BHARU DIARY

Two police jeeps drove us past the peaceful Malaysian countryside. Hidden behind the lush palm trees were wooden houses on stilts, also painted in bright colours like the villas at the lake resort. They reminded me of the pretty chalets in the enchanted world the Seven Dwarves and the Three Bears inhabited. I was experiencing an enchanting moment myself.

Others were also in high spirit. Everyone was laughing and making loud comments about the amazing scenery outside. The hot tropical wind that beat against my face felt like spring breeze.

We had a short rest at a police station. The officers must have been notified beforehand of our arrival. They had buckets of fresh milk and loaves of sweet bread waiting for us. Could there be anything that tasted as nice!

After a short rest we climbed back into the jeeps and were told we would be driven to 'Kota Bharu'. The exotic name did not mean anything to me, but I was sure that even if we were told that we would be going to another planet, we would still be cheering with glee. We were now safe from the Communists. We had reached the shore of freedom. That was all that mattered.

The further we travelled, the more desolate the landscape became, until all that I could see was an ever expanding sandy plain. Suddenly, in the middle of nowhere, a lonely structure appeared. It was a fenced compound consisting of several wooden barracks. In stark contrast to the lifelessness around it, this place was teeming with people.

Our jeeps stopped outside the locked gate. The camp inmates flocked towards the gate. Those at the front pressed their bodies against the chicken-wire fence, their intense gazes fixed on us.

Many of the men and boys only had a pair of tattered shorts on, their bare chests glistening with sweat. Some looked wild, with long and unruly hair brushing their shoulders, yet there was something fragile and haunting, like deep sadness, in their eyes.

It took me a moment to realise these strange-looking people in this harsh setting were my Vietnamese compatriots. Their skin had darkened significantly because of the burning sun. They looked like a lost tribe in the Sahara desert.

I was about to join them.

What was awaiting me behind the fence, I wondered apprehensively.

I got off the jeep, but almost jumped back immediately. The sand was so hot. The moment I stepped on it, the soles of my feet were burning. Like the rest of the group, I had lost everything to the sea, including my slippers. The clothes on my back were my only possession.

The gate of the compound opened for us to pass, then it was closed and locked up again. People inside the camp approached us in droves. A group of Malaysian officers, some in civilian clothes, some in army uniforms, strode towards us. People made room for them, then formed a quiet circle around us. They seemed quite respectful towards the Malaysians.

We were told to sit on the ground. The heat from the sand seeped through the thin material of my pants. I thought the skin on my bottom would peel!

A Vietnamese man stood next to the Malaysians to translate for them. He wore a pair of shorts as well as a collared shirt. This set him apart from the mainly bare-chested men and gave him a respectable look.

The stern-voiced Malaysian in charge of the camp talked in English. The Vietnamese man translated:

'You have entered Malaysian territory illegally. As such, you have committed an offence against Malaysian law. Malaysia, as a country, will treat you humanely. However, during your stay in this camp, you are required to observe the rules as set out by the camp authority. You are to respect order and conduct yourselves in a responsible manner. Those engaged in unruly conduct will be severely dealt with.'

I looked at my escape companions. Their exuberance since we were allowed to land had been dampened somewhat. Mrs Chung must be disappointed. There was no crowd of Western journalists assembling here to welcome the heroic people from Vietnam who dared risk their lives crossing the sea for freedom, as she had proudly predicted.

From the way we were treated, I sensed that these Malaysian officers considered us as nothing but an unwanted burden.

The Malaysians left. The Vietnamese interpreter stayed back and introduced himself to us:

'I am one of the camp coordinators. My name is Tung.'

We stood up, not quite sure what we were supposed to do.

'Well...welcome to the shore of freedom.' Tung uttered this grand statement in a low-key, almost apologetic manner. It was the apt thing for him to say, for the occasion deserved celebration, but it was clear to everyone that the confronting condition of the camp presented yet another challenge.

'Can I have a few young men to pitch a tent for these people?' Tung asked the crowd. Many raised their hands.

'How long was your trip?' he asked Tin.
'Seven days,' Tin said.
'Which escape route did you take?'
Everyone in the crowd seemed to have a question for us.
'Rach Gia.'
'You are from which region?'
'Dalat.'
'Did you encounter the pirates?'

Already I felt a sense of friendship and closeness in this refugee community, a special bond between those who had been through the most incredible experience of their lives. The familiar world of a dear country that meant everything to us, that we loved until our hearts ached, had been destroyed. We now found ourselves nomads in a strange land. We were grateful to be given a temporary safe haven, even though this location seemed to be as remote from civilisation as possible. We were quarantined and isolated, but luckily we still had each other.

My group followed Tung past a row of wooden barracks. There must have been about a hundred people in each of them.

He stopped at a clear area near the back of the camp.

'Well, this area is big enough for a big tent.'

A team of male volunteers, including the boys from my group, started pitching a tent for us.

An elderly lady came out from the crowd and approached me. I greeted her with a respectful nod. After a short silence, she asked me in a quiet voice:

'Niece, were you...?'

For Vietnamese, the titles 'uncle', 'aunty', 'brother' or 'niece' are not only used among family members, but also to address unrelated people, depending on their age, as a mark of courtesy and respect. This lady addressed me as 'niece' because I was her niece's age.

I didn't quite understand what she intended to say.

'You know, some girls were... They could not even walk... They had to be carried...'

Her face displayed many emotions—care, concern, dismay—that I could not discern at the time. She disappeared back into the crowd. Her hair was rolled into a bun, she dressed in a simple black top and a pair of black satin pants, the typical outfit for Vietnamese elderly women. She would look perfect in a background of green rice fields and brown thatched huts—the classic depiction of a Vietnamese rural scene—but she seemed so out of place here. How out of place we all were.

I wished I could turn back the clock, rewinding it to the time when everything was normal and made sense to me. Our presence here, and the mangled fate of our country that had brought us here, seemed to defy logic.

The elderly lady reminded me of my mother.

My heart suddenly ached. My dear mother was so far away from me now. Mother, you can never imagine what your children are going through!

The families of Mrs Chung, Tran and Tam were all given a place in one of the barracks. The rest of my group shared the newly pitched tent.

We were overwhelmed by people's kindness. They came, one after another, to give us presents such as chopsticks, spoons and plastic bowls. These worn and used eating utensils were precious in this place. We were grateful because, like the majority of the refugees, we arrived at the camp with nothing but the tattered clothes on our backs. Families generously shared with us their food ration of cooked rice and tinned sardines, our first meal on shore. We would have our own ration the next time the food truck came, which was once a week.

With everyone in my group having been given a place in the camp, we were considered settled. The crowd who came to see us in the hope that they would find someone they knew, or at least someone who knew someone they knew, or came from their town or city, had now dispersed.

I stood outside our tent looking around.

After seven days at sea, as exhilarating as unwavering hope, as uplifting as the call of freedom, as frightening as the hovering of death, this harsh setting behind wire fences was not quite what I had envisaged as my destination.

And yet I felt happy and peaceful.

Perhaps, deep in my heart, the voice that had urged me to flee my homeland was telling me I was on my way back—to humanity.

'People from the boat 'Freedom'! You can go to the storeroom now to get new clothes, two items of clothing for each person,' the storekeeper said.

We followed him to the storeroom. It was a wooden hut in the middle of the camp. The man unlocked the door. A strong smell of old clothes rushed out. The entire surface of the hut was covered by a soft mountain of clothing. We literally climbed on it, lifting this piece and that piece, having fun at picking up the clearly quirky ones to throw at each other:

'Hey! This suits you!'

I chose two dresses. One had a hole towards the hemline the size of the palm of my hand, perhaps because mice had gnawed on it, or because its original owner had forgotten to turn off the iron, but it fitted me perfectly.

For the camp population of well over a thousand, there were only a few squat toilets for women and men. Those who built this camp could not have envisaged it would have to cope with this massive number of refugees. They were not alone. No one could have predicted the Communist takeover of South Vietnam in 1975 could have led to a human tragedy of this magnitude. The whole world stayed in shock as boatloads and boatloads of desperate men, women and children from Vietnam kept appearing on the high seas in search of a safe haven.

The hygiene of the camp was appalling. In the female squat toilets, faeces and urine were spilling out from the toilet holes, its floor ankle-deep with this foul mixture. The smell and the filth were unbelievable. I joined a long queue at the back of the camp to use the open latrines instead. They were simply a row of holes in the ground with wooden partitions between them. A barrier consisted of a few sheets of corrugated iron separating the toilet area and the rest of the camp.

We girls were desperate to have a wash. I could not wait to change into the clean clothes that I had just been given. The female washing area was also an open sky makeshift enclosure. Its walls consisted of a few crudely cut wooden slats; a plastic curtain was hung in the place of a door. The women squatted next to each other and washed themselves fully clothed.

There was a queue for everything and the washing area was no different. As soon as someone walked out, another person walked in. We borrowed a couple of buckets, went to the hand pump near our tent to fill them with water, then carried them back to the washing area to wait. It was already dark when our turn came.

As there was no drainage, the water that seeped into the sandy ground had nowhere to go, turning this area into a slushy swamp. Chunks of logs were placed on the ground for people to step and squat on.

I used both hands to scoop the water in the bucket and was about to splash it on my face and my neck when I heard a sniggering sound from above my head. I looked up. Sitting on the branches of a tall tree on the other side of the fence were three Malaysian men who were blatantly ogling at us. I could see the glint from their bulging eyes under the dark canopy. They clearly had no intention of disappearing and we were powerless to shoo them away.

We gave ourselves a quick splash, then left the washing area hurriedly. My dirty clothes were now clinging wet to my skin. I felt crushed at not being able to have a decent wash.

You know how important it is for a girl to look good and smell good.

We went back to our tent to change.

Only a week before, I had been staying in a hut in the middle of the vast rice fields of the Mekong Delta and got to see the beautiful countryside of my beloved country for the first time. Only the night before, I had been sitting on the deck of a Thai frigate, having just been rescued by the gentlemen of the Thai Navy. These changes of circumstance were so drastic, I struggled to grasp the extraordinary reality of it all. Was it true that I had just crossed the sea and left my country for good? Was I dreaming?

The majority of the camp population had retreated into the barracks, collapsing on their plank beds from the heat and the strain of the day. Those who could not sleep, or loved tranquility, took a stroll around the camp, relishing the night's cool and pleasant temperature.

I wandered to the other side of the camp with a bucket in my hand. I had overheard that the pump there produced cleaner water. The water from the pump near my tent was yellowish in colour and smelled of sewage as it was close to the wash area and the toilet area.

I walked past a few small gatherings. People sat in small circles on the ground talking to each other in low voices. A few amorous couples hid themselves in discrete corners away from the watch tower floodlight, holding hands and kissing each other.

The atmosphere was so peaceful; it reminded me of Saigon's leisurely night life. The tragedies that had brought everyone to this place seemed like a bad dream.

I filled the bucket with fresh water and carried it to the concrete pavement of a barracks nearby to wash my hair. I tried to do it quietly so those sleeping inside were not disturbed.

As I was crouching and using a plastic cup to pour water on my hair, I felt a gentle tap on my shoulder. From behind the open window of the barracks, a hand reached out to me and pressed into my palm a bar of Palmolive soap, still in its golden wrap.

I let out a soft cry of delight at the surprised gift. Perfumed soap and everything refined and beautiful had disappeared from my life and the lives of other South Vietnamese since the Communist takeover. I had learned to live without it and tried to forget that it had ever existed, just as I had learned to suppress all desires for comfort and beauty, signs of bourgeois decadence. The new, supposedly more idealistic society glorified self-sacrifice and self-denial for a greater cause. A regime that could only deliver war and poverty needed to drum up these values. Now that I saw that bar of Palmolive soap again, it was as though a natural part of life had come back to me.

Its golden wrapping sparkled under the moonlight.

'Tha...nk you... Tha...nk you,' I stuttered, feeling overwhelmed holding such a precious thing in my hand.

It was the equivalent of a piece of gold in this place. It was a piece of gold to me. It was exactly what I craved for my hair.

I didn't have a home, I had lost my country, but at this moment my bad hair was my main concern. Girls being girls.

I lifted my wet hair up with my hands, turned around searchingly to look for my Samaritan so I could thank him or her. The mysterious person had quietly retreated back into the dark interior of the barracks.

The following morning, smelling luxuriously of perfumed soap, I went to that barracks and leaned over the window sill, shyly casting my glance around. No one from over one hundred people in there gave any indication that he or she was the person behind the previous night's kindly gesture. People were busy tucking into their breakfast.

I walked back to my tent. The smell and the sight of food had made me feel even hungrier. People were spreading thick layers of butter on their sandwiches or pouring sugar into their tea. The extravagant coffee aroma, the mouthwatering beef congee, the golden curly strands of instant noodles, they tasted even better in my imagination. Even in here, those with money did not seem to miss out on anything.

I sat outside the tent, putting up with the grumbling noises in my empty stomach and trying to act unaffected when Tung the coordinator approached.

He said the United Nations High Commission for Refugees (UNHCR) delegates were at the camp right now. They were in desperate need for interpreters to help them interview the refugees and process their applications for permanent settlement in third countries.

Tung had obtained the personal details of everyone in my group when we first arrived. He was impressed that many of us could speak French, some could also speak English.

My stepsister My and another girl, Van, volunteered for the interpreting jobs.

Subsequent to this, and perhaps as a reward for their volunteering for this important task, Tung got a place for all of us in the headquarter barracks.

The camp had ten barracks, each measured thirty by nine metres. The one we moved into was considered the camp's headquarters because all important activities seemed to be carried out there. It had a First Aid corner, consisting of an old single bed with a rusty metal frame and a thin mattress, and a tiny locked medicine cabinet with not much medicine in it, affixed to the wall next to the bed. Two doctors among the refugees provided care for the sick. The camp's coordinating committee often held meetings in the First Aid corner. They sat on the sick bed discussing important issues.

Three rows of wooden platforms ran the length of each barracks. The two next to the walls were of normal bed height, the one in the middle was only ankle high.

The high platforms were prime real estate. Those who had a place on the high platforms could rest their backs against the wall, enjoy the rare breeze that blew through the open windows and look outside for a change of scenery, even though that might only mean being able to watch the crowd outside instead of the crowd inside. Another great advantage for them, unlike the low platform dwellers, was not having to put up with people walking past, constantly flicking sand onto their faces and their food.

We were given a place on the low platform. This was a welcome change. It was many times better than sleeping in a tent on a nylon spread. The sand under the nylon spread was burning hot during the day, yet chillingly cold at night.

Each person in the barracks was allocated just enough space to sit up and lie down. You would be surprised to know how little space you need, if sitting up and lying down is all you do.

Interviews with the immigration officer from Australia were held in my barracks. The interviewer and the interviewees sat on long benches opposite each other across a wooden table. A big crowd surrounded them, observing the whole procedure with intense interest.

This morning Tung had given my group the application for permanent settlement forms to fill out.

'Which country you people want to go to?' he asked.

'America, of course,' My said.

For many South Vietnamese, America seemed an obvious choice. We were used to American GIs' presence on our soil during the Vietnam War. American culture was familiar to us. We had watched American movies, tasted American canned food, read American literature, as well as trash magazines. Many people attended English classes at the Vietnamese-American Association, learned to speak English with an American accent, and need I say it, it was America's betrayal of my country to the Communists that had triggered this mass exodus.

'Well, everyone wants to go to America; the American delegate has a huge backlog,' Tung said. 'They left just before your group arrived. It will be many months before they come again. Some who applied to go to America and refused to go anywhere else have been living in this camp for over a year now. They are still waiting. Choose America, if you wish, but be prepared for a very long wait. Do you have anyone in America to sponsor you?' he asked.

Seeing that we were totally ignorant about this, Tung explained:

'If you have a sponsor, that is someone who is willing to support you financially once you come to America, there is a greater chance that you would be accepted by the American delegate. Even then, the waiting list is still very long. If you don't have a sponsor, I suggest you apply with the French or the Australian delegate who are here right now. You are very lucky that they came yesterday, the day of your arrival. You have been spared the long wait.'

Even though everyone in my family could speak French, we did not apply to go to France. Our father went to Paris to study for two years. To save money he stayed in the cheapest apartment he could find in a shabby quarter where Parisians of modest means lived. 'Nothing is as glamorous as in the movies. There's dire poverty, even in France,' Father had told us.

At Tung's urging, we decided to submit our application for permanent settlement with the Australian delegate. This was the first time I had heard of Australia. I wondered where it was on the world map.

My family joined the crowd surrounding the interview table, waiting for our turn.

'Do you speak English?' the Australian officer asked each of us.

'Yes,' My and Ba said.

'Very little,' Tin, Linh and I said. Our high school rudimentary English did not prepare us for the off chance of actually using it to converse with a native English speaker.

'Why did you leave Vietnam?'

'If you lived with the Communists, you would understand why,' Ba replied.

The Australian smiled in sympathy.

Some people had forewarned us about the Australian delegates.

'The delegates from Australia are very fussy, very choosy. Australia looks after its refugees very well compared with other countries, but it's very hard to get accepted into the country in the first place.'

The gentleman's smile seemed like a good omen. Maybe he liked the way we filed in and sat down politely in front of him, in age order from left to right. Besides such a display of good manners and discipline, we did not have much else to show.

Against everything we felt appropriate, we turned up to the interview barefooted. We had donned our new clothes, courtesy of the camp's charity bin. They were in need of some ironing.

After a suffocating time under a dictatorial regime, the refugees in the camp had the chance to practice democracy again. Each barracks elected its own representative.

The barracks' representatives formed a coordinating committee to liaise with the Malaysian bosses, the UNHCR delegates and the immigration officers of different countries who came to the camp.

Democracy was that simple. Everyone had a say about how things were run and could raise their concerns or requests without fear. It made people happy. Problems could be brought out in the open. Shortcomings could be improved. Why did the Communists oppose it so vehemently?

A food truck came once a week, unloading bags of rice and cartons of sardines with the UNHCR logo on them to be distributed to the camp population. Those with money did not have to confine their diet to rice and sardines. A kiosk, located inside the camp next to the entrance gate, carried most things to make life easier for those with money: bread, instant noodles, snacks, soap, shampoo, washing detergents and cooking utensils. Merchandise not in stock could be ordered in, including all types of meat, except pork. Malaysia is a Muslim country and Muslims don't eat pork. A couple of locals drove their mini-trucks filled with fresh vegetables to the camp to sell daily. Others erected makeshift stalls along one side of the camp, on the other side of the fence, to sell snacks to the women, cigarettes to the men, and a million little things that people with spare change suddenly found necessary. The refugees, an unlikely group of consumers, had created a mini-boom for the local economy. Money passed through the holes of the chicken-wire fence, the goods went back the same way or were thrown over the fence.

A Malaysian soldier stood guard in the tall watch tower at one corner of the camp. His friendly manner and broad smile gave the refugees the comforting impression he was here only to maintain order and not to instill fear. His attitude reflected the humane attitude of the man in charge of this camp, a quiet and caring man named Zek.

Zek's office was a pre-fabricated cabin installed just outside the gate. To his and his staff's credit, they went about their tasks in a very low-key manner. The refugees were largely left to themselves, and to their credit, conducted themselves in a way that required very little interference from the Malaysian camp authorities.

Zek toured the camp daily, often with a Vietnamese representative by his side, who updated him on the camp's situation or interpreted for him when he wanted to talk directly with the refugees to find things out for himself.

A tall man with a heavy build, Zek did not project an imposing presence like those proud of their power and conscious of their own importance often do. He talked softly and always bent his head down to listen attentively to his short Vietnamese assistant.

Zek and his team saw their roles not as prison guards, but administrators of a humanitarian mission: to take care of the daily food supply, to oversee the living conditions in the camp and the general wellbeing of the camp population. To accommodate large groups of new arrivals in this already overcrowded camp with only makeshift facilities must have been a big challenge for them. Zek's caring attitude towards the refugees made me think the harsh living conditions were beyond his control, and he tried to alleviate them in the best way he could.

On our first night in the barracks, we did not have any blankets or mosquito nets. We draped our old clothes over our faces and our feet. They provided neither warmth nor protection against the vicious Malaysian mosquitoes.

Zek, on his routine night strolls, stopped right in front of us. We parted the rags onto the side, sat up and greeted him with embarrassing grins. He shook his head, clearly affected by what he saw.

'There are mosquito nets in the storeroom; how come these kids are not given any?' he asked the Vietnamese man who accompanied him.

The Vietnamese mumbled something about how we had only recently arrived and he had not had the time to deal with us yet. Zek frowned, clearly displeased. He and the man went to the storeroom right away and came back with a huge brand new mosquito net and a couple of light blankets. Zek made sure the mosquito net was properly propped up and we were nicely tucked in before he left.

Despite the surrounding fence and the fact we were not allowed to leave the place at will, I felt protected, rather than being placed under guard, thanks to Zek's compassion.

Father Maurice Surmon, a French priest of MEP (Societe des Missions de Paris), a Roman Catholic missionary organisation, was the chaplain of the camp and another refugee centre in Pulau Bidong. He came to my camp every Sunday to hold outdoor Mass for the faithful and provide help to all. The refugees adored him. Whether they were Catholic or not, he represented the forces of good, of kindness, and he was a source of spiritual comfort. For those who suffer, these are the very things they crave. There were many suffering people in that place. Their eyes brightened up and their faces lit up the moment the kindly priest drove his white van into the camp.

After Mass, Father Surmon would haul out bags of donated clothes from his van to the storeroom and hand the coordinators stacks of letters and money orders he had received from the refugees' friends and relatives to be passed on to them. He gave out aerogrammes to those who wanted to write to their loved ones and, occasionally, money gifts to the needy as well. He listened attentively to those who sought his personal blessings before leaving with the usual big bag of letters the refugees asked him to post for them.

As much as they adored him and were ever grateful to him, at the time no one fully realised the extent of his dedication and the extreme difficulties he had to overcome to be with them, and for them:

> *He had to risk his life in a boat ride to [Pulau Bidong] island through the treacherous estuary of Sungai Terengganu and the choppy waters of the South China Sea, especially daunting during the monsoon season. He had also put to good use all his diplomatic skills to get around the bureaucracy of the administration to bring much needed comfort and consolation to the refugees and to meet their spiritual needs. [He was] the fearless defender of their dignity.*[1]
>
> (Tribute to Father Surmon who passed away on 29 January 2009 at the age of 86.)

My group had been in the camp for a fortnight, subsisting on an unchanged diet of rice and sardines. Compared with the starvation Communist ration of sweet potatoes and Job's tears, rice and sardines were unbelievably luxurious. However, human beings are a fickle lot seldom satisfied with what they have, and so when we realised there was little chance the camp ration would vary in the foreseeable future, we decided to write to our relatives and friends overseas and ask for financial assistance.

With free aerogrammes from Father Surmon and borrowed pens from our sleep-site neighbours, we wrote begging messages, trying to word them as gracefully as we could.

While waiting for replies, we took turns to cook rice in a pot that was dented beyond recognition. It did not even have a lid. We covered it with a rusty sheet of corrugated iron and swallowed cooked rice mixed with tiny rust flakes.

Our wealthy Chinese neighbours on the high platform, whose daily occupation seemed to revolve around preparing and consuming delicious food, felt sorry for us and occasionally gave us their sardines ration. We thanked them profusely, but I wished I could have a taste of their exquisite Chinese cuisine instead.

This extended family of twenty-three members clearly loved and respected their patriarch. This elderly man with kindly eyes normally sat with his back leaning against the barracks wall, passing his time observing the multitude around him. His bare upper body, thick with several rolls of fat, gleamed with sweat. Almost always he would clutch a bamboo fan in his hand. It did not give him much respite from the oppressive heat, but he hung on to it, perhaps because it conveyed the comforting notion of coolness. Before the Communist calamity that befell our country, he could have been an all-powerful industry magnate. Now he looked gentle and benign, like the Laughing Buddha. The women talked to him softly and respectfully, and offered the food to him first.

Chinese migrants under the Vietnamese Communists were victimised for both their race and their class. After the Communist victory over South Vietnam, relations between

China and Vietnam turned sour. China supported the Khmer Rouge against Vietnam's occupation of Cambodia. Vietnam retaliated by conducting a brutal ethnic cleansing campaign against all Chinese in the country. The Chinese in South Vietnam were known for their entrepreneurial flair. Many owned successful businesses. The Communists confiscated their possessions, banned them from engaging in all trading activities, which for generations had been their main means to earn a living, then drove them out of the country. Government agents organised escape boats for them. The escapees under this scheme were called the 'semi-officials'. For a hefty fee in gold or cash, they were given the necessary papers to leave the sea borders of Vietnam without being bothered. This meant many of these people were being robbed blind again, then sent to their deaths. There was no guarantee that the boats provided were seaworthy. There was no guarantee that the escapes would be successful. Hundreds of thousands of Boat People never reached friendly shores.

Eating in the camp could be an enjoyable activity if one could temporarily ignore the appalling sanitary conditions. Out of necessity, and thanks to that wonderful survival instinct, people learned to block unpleasant things out of their minds so they could continue on with the joy and struggle of living.

The communal kitchen was only a short walk from the newly installed above-ground cesspools. These concrete, cylinder-shaped containers, over half a metre in height and one and a half metres in diameter, were recently hauled into the camp by trucks to replace the constantly overflowing toilets. They would be removed when full. Like many unsatisfactory arrangements in this place, the depressing proximity between the location where food was prepared and where body waste was excreted reflected the constraint of circumstances rather than a lack of common sense. Removable cesspools seemed to be the best answer for the severe lack of adequate toilets. The small clearing near the women's washing area seemed to be the most appropriate location for them. A short distance from the kitchen, this area had not yet turned into a swamp, but had been affected by the increasing volume of washing water that was poured out and remained stagnant underground. Its sandy surface was always soft and wet and could not be used for better purposes.

People stepped on to the platform of these concrete cesspools and squatted above a hole in the middle. There was neither wall nor cover to protect their modesty. The stench of human waste pervaded the whole camp. It bothered me initially, but then, like everything else in life that one could not change, I just had to get used to it. Until I left the camp, I had forgotten what clean air smelled like.

The maggots from the cesspools often crawled their way into the kitchen. Sometimes they even ventured into the barracks where people slept. At my first encounter with these tiny, plump and stark yellow creatures, I went cold with horror. Goosebumps covered my skin. They were another unpleasant thing I had to get used to. Whenever I saw them, I would simply use a stick to crush them.

I felt I surely deserved a big pat on the back for having managed to cope with all these trials and tribulations. Under normal circumstances, I would have found them insurmountable. I realised the survival instinct I had read about in books also resided in me. It seemed like a dubious blessing, as it only revealed its presence in times of harsh luck.

I wrote a cryptic letter to my parents to let them know their children had reached safe haven. I addressed them as 'aunty and uncle', not 'mother and father'. I did not want the security police to wave my letter in front of my parents' faces as irrefutable proof they were responsible for giving birth to traitors who betrayed the socialist motherland by fleeing overseas. I inserted some clichéd propaganda intended for the censors' eyes. I do not have a copy of the original letter. This is the gist of it:

> *October 1978, Kota Bharu, Malaysia*
>
> *Dear aunty and uncle,*
>
> *For a long time I haven't heard from you, I hope you and my cousins are all well. I have been living overseas for a long time, that's why I miss my home province very much. My brothers and sisters have moved to Malaysia to study and are currently living with me. I hope you still remember them (here I inserted our nicknames). All of us are trying to do well at school to make our parents happy. I remember with fondness the last time we went to Dalat to visit you both with our parents. We had such a wonderful time. Aunty, I really miss your beautiful cooking. I am very happy that our country is advancing towards socialism. I hope that one day I can go back to visit both of you again to see all the wonderful progress in our beloved country.*
>
> *Your beloved niece,*

It took many months for this letter to reach my parents. Until it did, my father had to stay strong for my mother. She was beside herself with the agony of not knowing whether her children were already dead or still alive. They also had to put up with the security police's constant harassment.

Father was summoned to their office several times. Each time, Mother feared it would be the last time she would see him alive. During the long hours of waiting, hoping her husband would come back, Mother would try to block the frightening vision that loomed in her head of him being handcuffed and led away by armed soldiers.

Among those who were taken away, some ended up in a shallow grave in Dalat's Catholic cemetery. This resting place for departed souls, since 'peace' time, had been desecrated and turned into a site of summary execution. Those living in its vicinity bowed their heads and cited a silent prayer for yet another victim every time they heard the sound of gun shots in the dead of night.

Jacqueline Desbarats estimated that more than 65,000 South Vietnamese citizens were executed after the fall of Saigon. This figure was later revised to approximately 100,000. Two thirds of the executions happened in the first two years of the new Communist government. These were all carried out in the name of 'national interests'.[2]

Before our escape, only my little sister Linh lived with my parents in Dalat. Her older siblings, including me, were already in Saigon.

The police kept grilling my father about her disappearance.

'What happened to your daughter? Where has she gone? Did she join those traitors who try to flee the country? Who instilled these subversive ideas in her head?'

'I don't know. I honestly don't know,' Father said.

'You are the parent, yet you don't know your daughter's whereabouts. What kind of parent are you?'

'I care for her; I raised her the best way I could. Now somebody came along, some bad friends came along and talked her into leaving her parents, what can I do? I have lost my daughter, she has failed to fulfill her filial duty to her parents, what can I do?'

In this small town, where everyone knew everyone, news travelled fast. Rumours travelled faster. Several kids had disappeared. A boat had capsized. No one survived. When did that happen? Which boat? Whose kids?

Mother almost went crazy with worry. 'What have we done,' she asked Father. 'We let them go because we want them to have a better future. There is no future for them here. But how can I continue living if my children are no longer alive? What happened to them? Why haven't we heard from them? Please, God, please, Buddha, I'm begging you. Please look after my children. I entrust them to you.'

I would love to tell my parents how well fed and well clothed we were at the camp. I would love to tell them that even destitute refugees like us were spared the chronic hunger and deprivation the Vietnamese population had to endure under the Communists.

I would love to assure them that, even though we experienced physical hardship, we also experienced human kindness. People of different nationalities, who spoke different languages and were total strangers, cared for us, looked after us, comforted us, and tried to find a place somewhere in the world for us so we could rebuild our lives.

How could we ever have survived without the kindness of strangers?

How could we ever thank them enough?

Just two weeks in the camp and already I had put on weight. So had my little sister. We spent the greater part of each day eating, sitting around and lying down at our sleep site. Strangers slept next to each other, separated only by an invisible demarcation line during the day and the flimsy wall of the mosquito nets at night. There wasn't much room to move. That sounds like a good excuse for my weight gain.

Thanks to hand-me-downs from those leaving for third countries and donations from the local people, our wardrobe improved. Occasionally we managed to pick up some really nice items from the camp's storeroom, perhaps from wealthy donors. Donning fashionable clothes while going barefoot, I could have been mistaken for a hippie at Woodstock.

The camp's population kept growing, from over a thousand when my group arrived to more than twice that number three months later. People of vastly different backgrounds learned to live right next to each other. I am proud to say I could not have been among a more decent group of people. Everyone tried their absolute best to treat each other with civility and kindness in the face of trying circumstances. Everyone was going through indescribable pain and loss. We understood and sympathised with each other.

There were only two rowdy incidents in the three months I was there. In one, two men got into a physical fracas over money. A man reneged on his promise to pay the balance of his due for the boat trip to the boat owner. In the other, a jealous wife came to my barracks armed with a long stick to look for a pretty single mother her husband was infatuated with. The camp coordinators were called. Thanks to their mediation skills, the warring parties were soon pacified.

There was no privacy in that place. The human comedy provided distraction, entertainment even, for the crowd. Everyone was privy to the open mediation sessions. A promise of repayment was made in one and marriage counselling was given in the other.

Vietnamese customs confined activities of a sexual or intimate nature to the couple's bedroom. There should be no amorous display in public. As a result, couples in the camp refrained from physical displays of affection towards each other. Perhaps against their will, abstinence was strictly observed. Young love birds waited for nightfall to find a discrete corner so they could hold hands or steal a kiss.

The challenge for everyone in the camp was to pass the time constructively while waiting for others to decide their fate. English classes were held in tents. The women taught each other to knit and alter clothes so they fitted better. In some other camps, auto mechanic classes were run to give the men a practical skill to help them find a job in their new homeland.

Chinese chess became popular when someone received a set in his gift package. It was such a good idea that other people went to the kiosk to order theirs.

Another form of entertainment in the camp that could compete with Chinese chess, in terms of popularity and crowd attraction, was the occasional performance by a suddenly inspired amateur singer. I would drop whatever I was doing to follow the crowd to a tent or a barracks where a heart-touching singing voice was coming from. The singer was often accompanied by a guitarist who played on one of the two guitars in the camp. These beautiful wooden instruments had survived the escape journey with their owners. They were much cherished by the camp dwellers and always in high demand. In this harsh environment, they represented something sweet, fragile and emotional, something soothing and comforting for many broken souls.

Hidden talents would reveal themselves at these spontaneous performances, bringing a smile to the audience's faces or reducing them to tears with well-known songs banned by the Communists. Like caged birds being let out to fly and realising they can spread their wings to soar in the sky, people rediscovered their freedom with a new sense of appreciation. Songs I had previously dismissed as corny, perhaps because I had never been in love, now rang so deep, so true, so humane to me.

> *She comes into my life*
> *In those wintry afternoons laden with sorrow*
> *When the foggy rain falls heavily on my shoulders*
> *When the dusty wind hurls through many skies*
> *When thick clouds descend on many seas*
>
> *She comes into my life*
> *When my soul shivers in freezing terrains*
> *When falling leaves drift in the air along autumnal streets*
> *When darkness falls in the land of forgetfulness*
>
> *She had come into my life*
> *How can she recall nothing of my love*
> *My darling, you had come into my life*
> *Did our love really leave no trace in your memory?*
>
> > 'Nguoi di qua doi toi' (She comes into my life)
> > Lyrics by Tran Da Tu
> > Music by Pham Dinh Chuong

The poet Tran Da Tu, a leading figure in South Vietnam's free, liberal and humanist literature, was the author of these lyrics. The Communists locked him up for twelve years for having produced this type of reactionary cultural product. The kind of love sanctioned in Communist Vietnam was the love for Uncle Ho, the Party, the working class and the country's noble mission to build a heaven for the proletariat. These notions were instilled in children's heads from infancy. Nursery rhymes were 'Last night I dreamed of Uncle Ho' and 'No one loves us little children more than Uncle Ho', not 'Twinkle, twinkle little star'. As romantic love hindered progress, those who incited romantic love were condemned as renegades.

In prison, Tran Da Tu was given the chance to learn the right way of thinking through political education and hard labour. Yet he still wove intolerable lyrics such as these:

> *The sun still sheds its golden light, even though I'm in the autumn of my life*
> *The sky is still blue, in spite of so many heartbreaks and devastations that came*
> *hurling down on me*
> *Poetic inspiration still comes to me*
> *Songs are still on my lips*
> *I still love her hair even though it has now turned grey*
> *No, it doesn't matter to me*
> *Like an old cherry tree that never ceases to blossom*
> *I belong to you*
> *My love for you will never end.*
>
> 'Vang trang xua' (The moon of long ago)
> Music and lyrics by Tran Da Tu

Tran Da Tu was deemed beyond redemption. His lengthy sentence reflected the seriousness of his crime.

His wife, the novelist Nha Ca, no doubt the inspiration for his passionate love poems, was also imprisoned. She wrote *Giai Khan So Cho Hue* (*Mourning Headband for Hue*), an eyewitness account of the massacre of thousands of unarmed civilians, including Catholic priests, Buddhist monks, civil servants, doctors, teachers, university professors and students by the Communists when they occupied the ancient imperial city of Hue during the 1968 Tet Offensive.

She was branded a cultural aggressor.

***

There was added poignancy when I heard a song based on Huu Loan's famous poem in the refugee camp. His personal tragedy was also the tragedy of my nation.

Huu Loan's poem *Mau Tim Hoa Sim* (*The Purple Hue of Rose Myrtle Flowers*), a moving tribute to his first wife who died an untimely death, brought him fame.

> ...
>
> *She often wore purple*
> *The colour of rose myrtle flowers*
> *In quiet nights*
> *Sitting beside an oil lamp*
> *Lovingly, tenderly*
> *She mended the torn shirts for me*
> ...
> *I'm crossing hills of rose myrtle flowers*
> *On my way to the battlefield*
> *At dusk*
> *Hills of rose myrtle flowers that spread forever*
> *In the twilight that lingers forever*
> *This forsaken place bathes in the purple shade of rose myrtle flowers*
> ...

Purple love letters to you I write
Purple tears I cry
Purple songs I sing
In the midst of rose myrtle flowers

The troop is on the move
To the upbeat sound of the horn
The dying sun emits a ghostly glow
A haunting, hovering image follows
Deep into the forsaken twilight of purple shadow

I call out her name
Where is she now
I want to reach out to her
Where is she now
My darling, my dearest
My worn shirt has not yet been mended...

Handsome, talented, French educated, Huu Loan typified the fine Vietnamese men and women who embraced the ideals of national independence and anti-colonialism when the country was under French occupation. He was among the first participants in the Viet Minh movement, the Ho Chi Minh-led anti-French resistance. Following the French defeat in 1954, the country was divided into Communist North, backed by China and the Soviet Union, and Capitalist South, backed by America. Huu Loan chose to stay in the North.

Once gaining control of the North, Ho revealed his true colour. A brutal Communist dictatorship was imposed on the North Vietnamese. Egged on by Stalin and Mao, Ho plunged the North in a bloodbath of 'Land Reform'.

An army of Chinese advisers came to North Vietnam to supervise the mass killing. Over 172,000 innocent peasants died. This was the official figure, released fifty years after the crimes were committed.³ The real death toll could be much higher. Overzealous cadres were keen to exceed the five per cent compulsory killing quota.

According to a 1937 survey, there were 965,000 landlords in North Vietnam, 882,000 of whom held less than 5 *mau* (1.8 hectares, or 4.5 acres) of land.⁴ Such small landholdings in a backward, war-ravaged and impoverished nation put them in the category of criminal exploiters. How many of them survived the massacre?

Official histories have since admitted that the majority of the victims of land reform were 'wrongly classified'.

Huu Loan and many veterans of the recent anti-French patriotic war realised that their patriotism had been hijacked by the Communists.

He and other writers, artists and intellectuals in the North voiced their opposition to the authority's outright attack on freedom of the press, freedom of expression and democracy in two literary magazines Nhan Van (Humanity) and Giai Pham (Masterpieces). The authority unleashed a terror campaign against them. Leaders of the movement, dubbed the Nhan Van - Giai Pham movement, were locked up for years. Contributors to these magazines were shunned from society and lived the lives of outcasts for the rest of their days.

Perhaps thanks to his fame, Huu Loan escaped the harsh punishment meted out to his fellow creative artists. His poem, however, was attacked for being 'reactionary'. 'At that time, if you wanted to write poetry, you had to write about Communism, about Uncle Ho; you were not allowed to cry or express your own sorrow,' he later explained.⁵

***

In one of Father Surmon's regular and much anticipated visits to Kota Bharu camp, he gave out pens and notebooks. My little sister Linh and I could not contain our excitement. We started our diaries right away.

We both had acquired the good habit of keeping a journal since high school. After the Communist takeover, we continued with it, except that we had to learn the art of self-censorship. The security police could come to people's houses to conduct a search at any time and for whatever reason. We took care not to reveal our real thoughts and feelings in our diary entries. The truth was either implied, disguised, or suppressed altogether. Sometimes I could not contain my emotions and would let them flow uncontrollably through the pages of my diary. Luckily, after such outpouring, I would quickly regain my good sense. I knew that any expression of dissatisfaction about our 'wonderful' socialist society had the potential to harm not only me, but also my family. The incriminating pages would be ripped out very rapidly and then burnt, or used as toilet paper.

I have relied a great deal on my little sister Linh's camp diary, and mine, in the writing of this memoir. Our recording of day-to-day events from over three decades still breathes the immediacy of the moment and helps me relive this extraordinary episode of my life.

Linh created her own challenge by penning her entries in French. My older sister Ba, a French teacher, corrected her grammar.

I started my diary, as well as a songbook. I wrote down the lyrics of all the banned songs, including the children's songs, the love songs, and the love poems that I could remember.

I felt like I was collecting the remnants of a lost culture. With only a pen and a notebook, I set out for myself a rather serious task—to preserve my country's cultural heritage that was being brutally destroyed in my homeland.

I asked people in my group and my new friends in the camp to assist me with this task. My collaborators and I would spend some time with each other, letting ourselves be mesmerised for a short while by the gentle world of feelings and imagination in the verses of a poem or the lyrics of a song. He or she would cite them for me to copy down, or better still, write them down for me. Quang Dzung's poem about love from a distance helped me momentarily forget the harsh reality of camp life:

> *Thương nhớ ơ hờ thương nhớ ai*
> *Sông xa từng lớp lớp mưa dài*
> *Mắt kia em có sầu cô quạnh*
> *Khi chớm thu về một sớm mai*

> *I miss you, I love you, a certain someone*
> *When the rain keeps falling on a faraway river*
> *Your eyes, I wonder - would your eyes sadden because of loneliness*
> *When autumn comes one bright early morn*

Or a poem by Jacques Prevert – my favourite French poet:

> *...et il est parti*
> *sous la pluie*
> *sans une parole*
> *sans me regarder*
> *ma tête*
> *dans ma main*
> *et j'ai pleuré*

> *...and he went away*
> *in the rain*
> *without uttering a word*
> *without looking at me*
> *I held my head in my hands*

and broke down in tears

A man turned on his cassette player day and night, providing my barracks with non-stop entertainment in the form of mushy songs about unrequited love and heartbreak. In normal situation, this could be grounds for complaint, but for we refugees, to hear these banned songs again was a joy. This was among the privileges of living in freedom that we had risked our lives for. I wasn't sure whether this man had managed to escape with his collection of forbidden music intact or his overseas friends had sent it to him. I furiously transcribed the lyrics in shorthand at first, then reproduced it in longhand. I vaguely sensed that these songs and poems would be of great comfort to me one day, when my only link to my lost country would be my memories, and no matter how happy I would be in my new homeland, that sense of loss would always leave a hole in my heart.

This self-assigned task brought me immense joy. If I had not kept myself busy in this way, perhaps I would have found it harder to cope with camp life.

When I left the camp, my modest songbook had become a three-hundred-page volume that even required an index.

It now occupies a special place on my bookshelf.

Vu, my brother Tin's friend, bound the songbook for me. Vu was particularly kind and thoughtful. One day he came to my site:

'Quynh, can I borrow your songbook?'

'What for? Do you have a song for me?'

'No. I don't have a song for you. But can I take it away?'

I looked away, not wanting to respond to his request. I didn't want to part from my most cherished possession.

'Come on. I'll take good care of it,' Vu pleaded.

'All right. Keep it very clean for me. Only handle it with your clean hands,' I emphasized the word 'clean'. He could see from the frown on my face how reluctant I was to see it out of my sight.

He returned it to me in the afternoon.

I exclaimed in delight. Vu had cut out a page with the picture of two lovers on horseback from a fashion magazine to make a cover for my songbook. He added another layer of transparent plastic to give it extra protection.

I was moved by his thoughtfulness.

One sweltering afternoon, I had just woken from a nap and was lying idly on the low plank, purposefully prolonging my rest to fill the day. People walked past, flicking sand onto my hair and my face. Vu came over.

'Quynh, try this.'

He sat down next to me, holding a tiny invention in his hand; he had transformed a few empty aluminium sardine cans into a miniature fan. The cans had been flattened and then shaped into rotating blades.

He put the tiny object close to my face, and, by some ingenuity, could make the blades move.

'Do you feel the fresh air?' he asked.

Vu wrote these lyrics of a French pop song for my songbook:

> *Je t'aime, et je t'aimerai toujours*
> *De l'aube a la fin des jours*
> *I love you, and will always love you*
> *From the break of dawn till the end of each and every day*

Vu was like another brother to me. Looking back, I wonder if Vu had more than brotherly love for me.

My diary recorded a continuous inflow of new arrivals during my stay in Kota Bharu camp:

24 November 1978 (Almost three weeks after our arrival)

Yesterday five hundred and eighty 'semi-official' escapees arrived. Tonight, another forty .The camp coordinator said that there are currently thirty refugee boats already in Malaysian waters seeking asylum. He thinks the camp population will likely increase to ten thousand. If that's the case the hygiene conditions here would be absolutely terrible.

1 December 1978

Yesterday another group of 'semi-officials' came, bringing the camp population to nearly three thousand. These people said that officers of the Malaysian Navy had beaten them up, and at first they were not allowed to land. The local Malaysians had also bashed and robbed them. The first case of typhoid fever was detected, but there is no medicine for it. People are swamping this place yet only few toilets are usable, the rest are blocked. The future doesn't look bright to me.

3 December 1978

Last night a group of one hundred and twenty five people arrived. One hundred and seventy five of their boat companions have died; the majority of the deceased were young Vietnamese who fled the country to avoid being sent to the battlefield in Cambodia. I wonder if any of my friends are among them. It's so, so sad.

The camp dwellers were asked to squeeze up, again and again, to make room for more people. No one complained. More people meant longer queues, but this also meant that more of their fellow countrymen had survived the treacherous journey and reached safe haven. I discovered that lying on my side instead of on my back did make a difference. I came to the conclusion that human flesh is malleable. That was the only logical explanation for the fact that this already filled-up-to-the-brim place could just keep on taking in more and more people. More tents had been set up.

As the camp population almost doubled in just a few weeks, the hygiene situation worsened. People stood under the punishing sun waiting for their turns to use the toilets, the water pumps, or to have a wash. New makeshift wash stations were erected along the concrete pavements of the barracks; each wash station consisted of a plastic curtain hung loosely on rough wooden frames affixed to the barracks' external walls.

The original wash area was now unusable. Some abominable souls had sneaked into it to relieve themselves.

The camp's coordinators gave pep talks calling on people's conscience and their sense of community. But clearly, had there been enough toilets, this foul behaviour could have been avoided.

I postponed having a wash or going to the toilet for as long as I humanly could. Head lice made a nest in my hair.

Other than these inconveniences, I was relatively fit and healthy throughout my stay at the camp. Given my history of ill health since childhood and the camp's harsh conditions, I was at a loss to understand my capacity to withstand hardship.

The camp management announced two cases of typhoid fever had been detected. Soon after the announcement, a most embarrassing situation happened outside my barracks. For a couple of days, there was the sorry sight of two young men, each sitting on a big plastic bucket placed on the pavement, their pants pulled down to their knees. No one knew whether they were the two people who had been inflicted with typhoid fever as had been announced or not, but clearly they both suffered from a dreadful bout of diarrhoea. There were not enough toilets in the camp. To give these poor men the exclusive use of two toilets for as long as their bowels were wreaking havoc was out of the question. Even if they had typhoid fever and should be quarantined, there were no facilities for this.

Sensitive to their plight, the crowd made sure not to act inappropriately and to carry on as normally as they could around them. The men's predicament could befall anyone in the camp. A water pump where people drew water for cooking and drinking was only a few metres away from where they sat!

Typhoid fever is a bacterial infection caused by the consumption of food and water contaminated with particles of human sewage. This place was an ideal breeding ground for it.

Luckily for the camp population, the spread of this serious illness did not eventuate.

Less than a month after our interview with the Australian delegate, my family was told that we had been accepted by Australia. The Australian bureaucracy was amazingly efficient. The rare smile from the Australian official who interviewed us, and was known to be choosy and difficult, had clearly been a sign of approval.

Yet we were still in two minds about Australia.

Some of our friends had been sponsored by their relatives in America. We would love to join them. Wouldn't it be nice to have the company of your friends when you were lost and lonely in a new country?

However there was no sight of the American delegate.

'What if we refuse to go to Australia?' Tin asked a coordinator.

'Well, you will be blacklisted and your application will go to the bottom of the pile. You are expected to accept the first offer of permanent asylum from any country. Beggars can't be choosers. Some of those who refused to go anywhere but America have been languishing in this camp for over a year.'

As Most Reverend Vincent Long mentioned in the foreword, the terrorist events of 11 September 2001 changed many people's perception about asylum seekers and refugees.

In 2016, Australia decided to adopt a much tougher approach towards asylum seekers, especially those who arrive by boat.

I recall the outpouring of international sympathy towards the Vietnamese refugees nearly four decades ago and realise just how incredibly lucky we were.

Wonderful countries that belonged to the free world, including America, Australia, France, Switzerland, Sweden, Germany, Belgium, Austria, Britain, Norway, Italy, Canada, Denmark, Netherlands, Finland, New Zealand, Japan, gave us the chance to apply for permanent asylum. Even the tiny nation of Israel opened its heart to us.

My family held an urgent meeting to decide whether we should accept the offer for permanent settlement in Australia.

'So what are we going to do?'

'I'm not sure if I want to stay too long in this place. It's hard enough having to share space with three thousand people in the camp. How are we going to cope with thousands more?'

'Where is Australia?' I asked.

'It's near New Zealand,' Ba said. She was the most knowledgeable among us.

'Where is New Zealand?'

'Remember Mrs Day's son? He received a scholarship to go to New Zealand to study.'

This simple fact reassured me immensely. It helped me draw a connection, albeit a very indirect one, between this strange and faraway country called Australia, and someone as close and familiar to me as Mrs Day, who was a neighbour and a good friend of my mother in the Geography Quarter in my hometown.

'Well, if Australia is close to New Zealand, it shouldn't be too bad then,' I reasoned.

Of course we were ignorant about the bad jokes that Australians loved to tell about their Kiwi neighbours.

Our brainstorming session, which virtually defined our future, went as deep as that. That was how Australia became our new homeland!

My family soon realised how very fortunate we were, having been granted permanent settlement in Australia at this juncture (November 1978). Malaysia had toughened its stance towards Boat People. In 1978, the Malaysian National Security Council established Task Force VII with the primary aim of stopping Boat People from landing. In 1979 boats carrying thousands of refugees were towed back out to sea. In June 1979 Deputy Minister Mahathir announced the 'shoot on sight' policy.[6]

At my camp, an ominous change in management reflected this shift in attitude towards the refugees.

Zek, the camp chief who was well liked and respected by the refugees, was replaced by a new tough man named Mohammed. He quickly made his authority felt.

One sweltering afternoon it was my turn to cook. I had been toiling over the coal stove in the communal kitchen, sweat beads running down my face. As I emerged from the kitchen to catch some fresh air, a sudden cessation of all noise in this part of the camp caught me by surprise. Silence was the rarest commodity in that place.

Everyone stood where they were. All conversation stopped. People turned their heads warily in the direction of a tall, angry man in khaki uniform and shiny knee-high leather boots. Like a horse-taming cowboy in the Wild West, Mohammed strutted along the main walkway, cracking his bullwhip indiscriminately at the crowd. Like a hissing snake, the whip made a whoosh sound every time it slithered ferociously in the air. Those who happened to be within its range scrambled left and right to save themselves.

Mohammed always carried a whip when patrolling the camp. On this particular afternoon, he was extremely furious because he had spotted a man peeing furtively against a barracks wall. The toilet queue was too long and the man could not wait. After giving the man a good lashing, Mohammed continued his inspection tour and caught a group of young men playing cards. This riled him even more.

Previously, when Zek was in charge, no one was admonished for playing card games. Gambling is forbidden under Islam, however some young men in the camp played card games just for fun, to pass the time, as they had a lot of time on their hands. Zek was tolerant enough not to strictly impose Islamic principles on the camp's largely Christian and Buddhist population.

Mohammed was different. He seemed to derive great pleasure from intimidating the refugees. The card-playing men didn't know what serious trouble they had just caused for themselves and for the whole camp population.

That night, as usual, all the lights in the barracks went out at ten o'clock. There should be no talking inside the barracks after this time. Those who went outside for a stroll or to meet up with friends must keep their noise down.

I lay on the hard surface of the wooden plank waiting for sleep to come. I could hear my female neighbour's quiet breathing on the other side of the mosquito net. Occasionally our limbs would brush against each other. It was impossible to avoid this unwelcome bodily contact. We were literally too close for comfort.

Each barracks was designed to accommodate, at most, fifty people. More than three times that number were sleeping in it.

In my half-asleep state, my mind often wandered back to Dalat, my hometown. I would revert to my former self, the teenager who did not have a worry in the world, who slept in a comfortable double bed with her little sister, who enjoyed the freedom to move her limbs in whatever way she wanted in bed, who liked to snuggle against her sister for warmth. I wished my dream would never end because I felt safe and happy in it, but of course it did, and always abruptly, when my neighbour gave me a none too gentle nudge to prevent me from invading her personal space and annoying her further. I did not think she would be sympathetic about my dream. For a time I was clouded in confusion and had to pinch myself a few times to be sure this strange and dark place was my reality.

Suddenly I heard the sound of hasty footsteps. The neon lights in my barracks were switched back on.

'Wake up! Everybody, wake up! Urgent assembly!'

The camp coordinators moved hurriedly along the narrow walkways between the three sleeping platforms, tapping and prodding those who refused to budge.

'Please wake up! Urgent assembly! Mohammed's order!'

Herds of men, women and children, in various states of dishevelment, made their wary way towards the front yard.

The refugees sat on the bare ground under the pale moonlight. It was hard to believe that the burning sand during the day could change to numbing cold at night. No one dared make a sound. Mohammed was pacing furiously in front of the crowd. A few Malaysian guards spread themselves around.

I heard Mohammed's angry yelling in English, followed by the interpreter's subdued voice:

'You people are very lucky to be in this camp. Kota Bharu camp is the best refugee camp in the whole of Malaysia. Do you know where the other refugees were taken to? A deserted island in the middle of the sea! If you do not behave yourself, you will be sent there. The punishment for these men is a lesson for all of you. I won't tolerate any more troubles.'

The young men who had been caught playing cards earlier on that day were forced to kneel before the crowd. Their heads hung low in shame, their hands behind their backs. The guards shaved their heads, then gave them some mighty lashes.

After the punishment, the crowd was allowed back to the barracks. No one uttered a word.

I could not go back to sleep afterwards.

The incident really upset me. Perhaps because it had forced me to face up to something that was so painful, something that until now I had refused to acknowledge: the cold and hard truth about my new status, or more to the point, my new *non-status*—that of a refugee. It was still early days since I was forced to erase the whole of my former existence and begin everything anew from an unfortunate starting point. This new life as a nomad was as foreign to me as an out-of-body experience. I had not been able to internalise it yet. I still thought of myself and my fellow countrymen as normal people of decent background who fell into hardship through no fault of their own. I still expected to be treated normally, that is with common courtesy and respect. I did not see why our ill fate should give others the right to bully us and look down on us as though we were inferior human beings. Zek's compassion had helped me preserve my sense of self, but Mohammed had thrown cold water on it. He had traumatised us simply because he could. We were at his mercy.

I realised how powerless and vulnerable we truly were. I felt scared and just wanted to cry.

A group of newcomers said they had been beaten and robbed by the locals when their boat landed on the Malaysian shore. I thought their story was sad enough.

The following night another group came. Their boat, carrying over three hundred people, reached the shore but was shot at by the Malaysian Navy. It became caught in a severe storm and capsized. Only half the passengers survived.

The Malaysian government's solution to the Boat People tragedy was simple: shoot them and let them drown.

The survivors walked silently into the camp. Wrapped from head to toe in blankets, they moved like shadows, a parade of mournful eyes and gaunt faces. The people in the camp stood still to show respect.

A young boy among the survivors stumbled towards a barracks wall, then slumped on the ground. There he sat for the rest of the night, immobile, a blanket draped over his small frame, obscuring his face, the haunted face of someone who has been through horror.

There was something so tragic and fragile about him that it compelled people to leave him undisturbed; words seemed hollow and comforting gestures so inadequate when the pain was too great.

Eleven members of his family embarked on that ill-fated journey. He was the sole survivor among them.

From that tragic night, many people reported strange occurrences. Stories of apparitions abounded. People suspected the dead were still lingering in this place because they could not bear parting from their loved ones.

A man had lost his wife and his young child in that ill-fated trip. In the barracks where he slept, some said they had seen a faint shadow of a young woman with an infant in her arm hovering outside the window at night. Others swore they heard a baby crying from somewhere *out there,* at odd hours, in the desolate area surrounding the camp.

At night the air seemed colder. Sometimes a sudden chill caused my hair to stand up and gave me goosebumps. I wondered if it was just my imagination or some invisible presence had brushed past me. A walk around the camp when the lights went out was like a nocturnal visit to a cemetery. People burned incense sticks and placed them on windowsills, stuck them on the ground outside their tents or tied them to the wire fence near where they slept. The red tips glinted in the dark, the soothing smell pervading the whole area.

Vietnamese and Chinese use incense sticks to commemorate the dead and communicate with them. For now this was the only way these survivors could manifest their grief.

What could give them some comfort, even though they might not know it at the time, was that even though some governments had turned hostile against them, there were individuals who cared deeply for them and tried to help them in their own ways, sometimes at great personal cost.

Mr Jeon Jae-yong was one such individual.[7] One day in November 1985, his fishing ship was crossing the South China Sea when he saw a rickety boat crammed with ninety-six people. For four days since fleeing Vietnam, these desperate people had watched many ships pass, 50 in all, and none had stopped to help pull them to safety.

It was day four, the engine was dead, the boat stayed adrift, the ominous clouds of a tropical storm headed their way.

They watched the 51st ship pass, resigned to another disappointment. Ten minutes later, a miracle happened. The South Korean ship turned around.

After passing the refugees, Mr Jeon Jae-yong, the ship's captain, called the sailors together. It was against company policy to pick up Boat People, but Jeon told them he would take responsibility. After discussing the situation, the sailors told him they were with him.

The captain made a U-turn. He allowed the refugees to board, gave them dry clothes, fed them tuna and brought them to Busan, South Korea's second-largest city. They were saved but Jeon, who had worked for the shipping company Koryo Wonyang Corp for sixteen years, was fired for not following the rules.

He was later investigated many times by intelligence agencies and could not find another captain's job. He survived through his savings and by helping out at friends' businesses.

Nineteen years later, those he had saved wanted to find him. Peter Nguyen and his wife were among them. Nguyen had settled in the United States and worked as a medical technician in California. He enlisted his Korean-American colleagues in his quest. He told them, 'Mr Jeon is the reason why I live, and if I can, I want to see him again.'

They found him. A big reunion was organized for him and the passengers of that stricken boat in Santa Ana in 2004.

Nguyen told Jeon when they met, 'I won't forget you until I die.'

'It was with God's grace that we found the boat people and were able to save all of them. Even if a puppy was in the sea, I would have saved it as well, so it was only natural that I should save precious human lives,' Jeon said.[8]

Like Jeon, Norman Sloane, the captain of a British ship, the *Entalina*, also put his career on the line when he decided to help the refugees.[9]

The *Entalina* was a Shell tanker. In 1979 it rescued about 150 refugees, including nineteen children under five years old, from a sinking refugee boat. Seven of the passengers had previously been killed by pirates, or died of starvation or exposure. The *Entalina* brought the survivors to Darwin, Australia.

Darwin Waterside Workers, a workers' union which sympathised with the Vietnamese Communists, went on strike in protest, saying the *Entalina* would not be allowed to leave Darwin if the refugees were allowed to remain in Australia. Action was also threatened against all Shell ships and any ships that dared to rescue Vietnamese refugees. Any ship's captain that did so could be seen as putting his career in danger.

Many passing ships simply ignored the refugees' distress signals. One of the survivors on the *Entalina*, Mrs Cam Ha, said:

'If the British ship had not stopped, we would be dead. Twenty-two ships passed us by and we waved and put up white flags, but they did not stop.'

Interviewed on ABC radio, Captain Norman Sloane said:

'How can we turn away from people in distress? It is impossible. As we approached we saw that there were obviously many people on board the ship. I saw one woman lift a child in her arms, and we knew that we had to take the greatest care to get her aboard ... I could only try my best. The first persons I saw were the children ... I would rather not say the feeling I felt when I saw those children. Well, I said to this little girl, "Were you afraid?" and she said, "No, I have done nothing wrong in my life and I knew God would save me." And then I felt, well then, my God, if that lass can go through the valley of the shadow of death and think that, then I can do everything I can to save them.'

Mr Yahao Alcoh Wong was another great benefactor of the Vietnamese refugees.

In 1978, an uninhabited island in the Malaysian state of Terengganu called Pulau Bidong was transformed into a reception centre for Vietnamese Boat People. Mr Yahao Wong was among its first volunteers.

From then on, he dedicated his life to these unfortunate people . Whenever he heard of another sunken boat being washed ashore, he would travel to the site, even in the middle of the night, to collect the bodies of the deceased. Before arranging for their burials, he had the foresight to record their personal details, as many as he could, knowing how important these details would be in helping surviving relatives identify their loved ones in the future.

Mr Wong died in 2006. His parting gift to the refugees was a book titled *The Guidebook of the Graveyards of the Vietnamese Boat People (VBP) along the East Coast of Malaysia Peninsula*. It contains the names of over 750 deceased boat people that he managed to collect and bury, along with the locations of their graves and other mass graves for unidentified victims.

Those whose bodies were picked up by Mr Wong were lucky, even though 'lucky' could never be the word to describe their fate, but at least their deaths, and by reference, their existence, were acknowledged. At least, thanks to this man's compassion and dedication to this harrowing task, some surviving relatives could finally put an end to years of living in a state of uncertainty, not knowing what had happened to their loved ones. Nothing could alleviate their sadness, except the sadness of knowing seems to be more bearable than the sadness of not knowing.

Of several millions of Vietnamese who fled the country, it is estimated over half a million have disappeared without any trace, presumed drowned. Thousands were murdered or kidnapped by Thai pirates. Those who received no news of their relatives since their escape would have to deal with the trauma of unresolved loss for the rest of their lives.

'Man is a creature that can get accustomed to anything'. Dostoevsky's remark sounds ominous. There would be many challenges in life, *anything* can happen; there is no point resisting. Be prepared. Eventually one would get used to even the worst of circumstances. Is this what he meant?

Since my escape I had been able to withstand anything and everything life had thrown at me. My ability to survive, and that of my fellow refugees, seems to have proven Dostoevsky's point. I wonder if man should feel triumphant or dispirited about this wretched ability—to be familiar even with heartbreak.

Dr Viktor E. Frankl, the founder of logotherapy and a Holocaust survivor, asserts that 'there is nothing in the world that would so effectively help one to survive even the worst conditions as the knowledge that there is a meaning in one's life'.[10]

It seemed the Vietnamese had found life without freedom had lost its meaning, and were prepared to risk everything, including life itself, in order to reclaim it.

For those who survived the escape journey, the air of freedom they breathed had given them the strength to cope with the harsh living conditions in the refugee camps.

For those who lay buried deep in their watery graves under the sea, those who were raped, murdered or kidnapped, and their surviving relatives, the meaning of freedom would forever be a dubious and ruinous concept. The price for freedom seemed to be nothing but savage extortion.

Freedom or death?

Freedom or perpetual slavery?

Death or perpetual slavery?
What horrible choices one had to make.

It was a day worth celebrating when Tin's friends, Ban and Vu, each received a gift of US$100 from their relatives overseas. They generously spent their small fortune not just on themselves but on the rest of the group. After one long month of having only cooked rice and tinned sardines for meals, it was nice to see some variety in our diet.

We had soup for a change. The ingredients for this 'special' soup included instant noodles, the soup powder in the instant noodles packet, and a bunch of spinach. The cooking method for this concoction was to put all said ingredients into a pot of boiling water and stir them all up. Normally one packet of instant noodles represented one serving. By adding water, salt and a bit of green, all eighteen of us could have a taste of instant noodles.

We also had sweet bread. The taste of sweet bread brought such joy to my palate. I marveled at every mouth-watering element of the dome-shaped bun the size of my palm before savouring it slowly and carefully, one small portion by one small portion, so it lasted longer. I did not chew; there was no need to be greedy and hasty. I let each pinch melt in my mouth, but not before having an appreciative look at it: the soft crust's subtle brownish colour sprinkled with shiny grains of sugar, the light and fluffy white inside slightly moistened by crumbs of golden butter, soft as a dream. Sweet bread should be among mankind's most amazing creations, I would be happy to declare!

There was even some money left for perfumed soap to wash our hair and detergent to wash our clothes.

My brother Tin came up with the idea of making bean sprouts. This fresh vegetable would be a welcome supplement to our dreary ration and hopefully a source of income, if he could sell it to other camp dwellers. Ban and Vu were happy to provide capital for this mini-venture; the main production requirements simply consisted of a bag of dried mung beans and a container.

Growing bean sprouts is simple. All you need to do is place a layer of dried mung beans on top of a layer of sand in a container, and repeat this until the container is full. The mung beans need watering every day and the container should be covered with a damp cloth to preserve humidity. After five days, fresh young shoots burst out of the seeds. They need to be rinsed thoroughly to get rid of the sand, after which they are ready to eat.

There were customers for the bean sprouts. Tin and his friends made some profit. My group had sweet bread and instant noodles for soup more regularly.

Other people came up with more elaborate money-making ideas. The vibrant Vietnamese shopping strips that would spring up in many foreign cities around the world in decades to come, could have been envisaged from the lively little economy that was growing in this refugee camp.

Some resourceful housewives set up squat stalls to sell their home-made cakes; there was a little cafe consisting of a makeshift coffee table and four tiny stools fashioned from leftover timber which had been used to build the barracks; an eating place with one wooden table and two wooden benches that served traditional Vietnamese hot food. The familiar voice of a well-known South Vietnamese singer lamenting about lost love coming out from a cassette player nearby provided constant background music.

It was as though a piece of sweet old Saigon had been saved from destruction and tentatively reinstalled in this faraway place.

I would love to say the special bond between members of my group, friends who had been with each other through thick and thin, through life and death on this most extraordinary journey, would never break. I wished I could say that our love for each other remained strong, despite all the hardships. Unfortunately this was not to be the case.

Ban and Vu used their money to buy food and necessities for the whole group, all eighteen of us. Their combined fortune of US$200 soon ran out. The modest profit from Tin's bean shoots venture had also been used to support the whole group. However, after a promising start, it was no longer viable. His bean shoots could not compete with the wonderful variety of fresh vegetables the locals brought into camp to sell every day.

We went back to the rice and tinned sardines regime.

Every time Father Surmon came into the camp with a new batch of mail, everyone would hope an envelope with a nice cheque in it would be addressed to them.

Several people in my group eventually received such good news. The rest of the group were happy for them. I felt quietly excited about an imminent improvement in my diet.

Up until this point, eighteen of us had shared every meal, every treat with each other. Each meal time was characterised by witty jokes, chatter and laughter, the kind of unreserved and spontaneous fun one enjoys among close friends. I certainly thought of everyone in my group as my close friends. The connection between us was special. How could it not be?

A good dose of reality would soon throw cold water on my tendency towards sentimentality.

Some of those I had thought my 'close friends' turned their back on the rest of the group the moment they had money.

The change in their attitude was swift, as swift as a short walk to the other side of the camp to get their cheque in the mail. They were still my friends when they went to collect their mail. When they came back, they avoided making eye contact with the rest of the group and looked for a corner away from everyone to sit down and munch on the tasty snacks they had just bought with their recent windfall.

The generosity of Ban, Vu and Tin had not been emulated nor reciprocated.

A weird division occurred between members of my group: those who had money and those who did not. Unfortunately my family belonged to the second group. So did Ban and Vu, my brother's good friends.

The 'haves' sat with each other at meal times and became distant and 'snotty' towards the 'have-nots'. I tried to maintain an amiable attitude with the 'haves'—after all, we had been friends—but realised very soon that my friendship was neither welcome nor wanted. I wondered if they saw my beaming smile as harbouring an ulterior motive - trying to gain their sympathy in the hope they would give me some food.

I came to the sad conclusion that if I came to think about my friends in this way, or if something had caused me to think of my friends in this way, then perhaps I had been trying to salvage friendships that were not worth salvaging. Perhaps it had never been there in the first place.

Perhaps I had read too many sentimental books. It was about time I learned to read people.

My group's sleeping arrangement had not changed. Boys slept with boys, girls slept with girls, at opposite ends of the barracks. A girl—I shall call her 'A'—who was a member of the 'haves' clique, only hung out with her moneyed friends now. She stayed at their sites during the day and only came back to the girls 'site at night to sleep. She lay next to me but we barely talked.

I could not hide my disappointment at the break-up of my group, especially at the disgraceful way it came about.

Tin noticed my long face:

'That's life, Quynh. Don't think too much about it. When you're more mature, you'll find that this kind of behaviour is just... normal. Very normal behavior,' he said.

His brotherly advice did not give me any comfort.

One day, another member of the 'haves' group—whom I shall call 'B'—complained he had lost some money. B had made some profit from selling bean shoots, but unlike Tin who used the money to buy food for the whole group, B only spent on himself.

'Someone must have stolen it,' B grumbled.

On that same day, Ban brought me and my little sister Linh to the cafe for a wonderful treat; we were shouted one glass of milk each. The boys—Ban, Tin and Vu—sipped coffee and smoked cigarettes. Ban appeared quite pleased with himself. He made a general comment, without referring to anyone or any incident in particular:

'That's the law of nature.'

I understood exactly what he alluded to.

The Vietnamese Communists often used the expression 'the law of nature' to justify the killing and pillaging of their own people. The uprising of the proletariat against the proprietor class by violent means was within the law of nature. To kill or rob those who were wealthier or more successful than you was within the law of nature. If you think communism is similar to the criminal codes, you are not wrong.

I had a tummy full of milk and found the 'law of nature', in this instance, worked very well for me.

No wonder communism appealed to the destitute.

It was finally my family's turn to have good news. To our immense relief, a cousin in America sent us a cheque for US$200.

It never rains, but it pours, and now money poured in from various sources for the 'have-nots'. Ban and Vu received another tidy sum from their relatives. Xuan, my sister Ba's good friend, also found a cheque in her mail.

What were we going to do with all this money?!

Of course we were going to do a lot of things with it.

Vu took my little sister Linh and me to the makeshift cafe for an exquisite gastronomic experience. It featured refreshing soft drinks and mouth-watering slices of buttered sandwiches sprinkled with sugar. The cafe was just a stroll from one end to the other end of the camp, but to sit on its rickety stools and be served courteously by its lady owner still felt special.

My family and our good friends were not exactly rolling in luxury, but there was now plenty of sweet bread—and it wasn't just for breakfast! Milk with a few spoons of Ovaltine before bedtime; instant noodles, perfumed soap, toilet paper, rubber thongs and—drum roll!—underwear for the girls! This was definitely cause for celebration. I felt part of civilised society again.

Now that we, the 'have-nots', were no longer destitute, the 'haves' suddenly became friendlier with us. They offered us some of their delicious food and resumed talking to us, perhaps because they now considered us their equals.

I didn't know how to handle this kind of friendship. Something had broken irretrievably.

December 1978

Three days after Christmas, the camp authorities suddenly gave orders to close the kiosk and ban all food trucks.

The kiosk and the food trucks had been the camp's lifeline. They supplied fresh food, vegetables, and all the necessities that made camp life more bearable. To the camp dwellers, they represented a link between this godforsaken place and the outside world. They brought the excitement of a village market to this dreary place. The Malay vendors, dressed in colourful sarongs, always smiled from ear to ear. Their tanned skin made the white of their teeth sparkle even more. They seemed more than pleased to see their merchandise snatched up by the crowd so quickly. Their absence was sorely missed.

The makeshift stalls on the other side of the fence were also subject to the trading ban.

Tung, the coordinator, returned to my barracks from a meeting with the Malaysian boss. He said Mohammed was very unhappy with the lack of discipline in the camp. This draconian measure would be in place until order was restored.

That was the official reason.

The real reason was someone had sent a letter to the United Nations to complain about the harsh conditions in the camp and the fact that the refugees here had been 'maltreated'. As a result the whole camp population was punished.

Some fingers silently pointed to a group of recently arrived 'semi-officials' for putting everyone in this predicament. The claim of 'maltreatment' could only come from them, people speculated. They were the lucky ones who'd had a smooth sea journey and had arrived with their possessions intact, including biscuit tins filled with gold. From the disgusted expressions on their faces, one could tell how shocked and appalled they were about the camp's living conditions.

'Well, we are not exactly holiday makers, are we? Who do they think they are?' someone asked sarcastically.

People's opinion about the anonymous complainer was split. Some saw him or her as a hero for daring to challenge the Malaysian authority and voice concern on behalf of the refugees. Others believed that, as refugees, we should *know our place*. We were now stateless and powerless. Our survival depended totally on other people's charity. We should count ourselves lucky just to be alive. We should be thankful for having been given temporary shelter in this camp. We could supplicate but were in no position to complain or make demands. What good in making a complaint? It only resulted in this trading ban that caused so much inconvenience to everyone.

The key obligation of the country signatories to the 1951 Convention and the 1967 Protocol on Refugees is to provide protection for asylum seekers and not to return them to the country where they fear persecution.

Malaysia is not a signatory to the Convention and the Protocol, yet it had opened its door to provide a safe haven for over a quarter of a million Vietnamese refugees. A whole island—Pulau Bidong—had been transformed into a rescue centre.

This act of immense generosity aside, the living conditions in many refugee camps in Southeast Asia were basic, primitive even.

In Pulau Bidong, people had to 'build their own shanties out of cardboard, plastic sheeting, hand-cut timber, bark and hessian bags. Human waste accumulated, attracting clouds of flies and packs of rats the size of cats'. [11]

In my camp, the lack of adequate toilets sometimes forced people, men and women alike, to squat down and relieve themselves in full view of the crowd, like animals. The confronting scene of those two men stricken with diarrhea stuck in my memory.

Malcolm Fraser, the late former Prime Minister of Australia, proposed 'the establishment of an international system of law that all countries, even the most powerful, will respect. This may be the greatest challenge to be faced in this century, but we have to meet it if we are to get a civilised community of nations'. [12]

Until such idealistic vision of the world becomes a reality, people will still be fleeing abuses in their own country; and the refugees problem would unlikely be eradicated.

At the camp, I was an ignorant eighteen-year-old teenager who had no idea what human rights were all about, or what rights refugees were entitled to. Until the 'letter of complaint to the United Nations' incident, the word 'maltreatment' had never entered my mind.

I counted myself lucky that I had not been pulled back to sea and left to drown. I had not been sent back to the oppressive regime that had driven me and my fellow Vietnamese to embark on this desperate journey in the first place. I was given a safe place to live. I was in the care of the world. I had a future to look forward to. I could not ask for more.

I felt blessed and immensely grateful.

At the same time, I wished I could leave the camp as soon as possible.

The shops had been a source of joy for the camp dwellers. Now they were all shut, this overcrowded place lapsed into something resembling quietude.

As people could no longer obtain cooking ingredients, the waiting queue at the kitchen to use the coal stoves had shortened. The wealthy Chinese family of twenty-three in my barracks used to monopolise several coal stoves every day to make sumptuous dishes. They seemed quite subdued now, as though they had lost their *raison d'etre*. I secretly welcomed this change. At least I would not have to put up with the beautiful aroma of their five-spice chicken or sweet corn soup, which had so often cruelly teased my taste buds.

Chinese chess was the unexpected benefactor of this trading ban. It had been a popular game in the camp before. Now it was a fad. Deprived of visceral pleasures, people turned to this cerebral past-time that Chinese and Vietnamese, whether commoners or nobility, in traditional or contemporary societies, all enjoyed.

The atmosphere in the barracks became much more graceful. Numerous pairs of bare-chested and sunburned Confucian scholars, in tattered shorts and rubber thongs, sat solemnly in lotus position opposite each other across a paper chess grid. Occasionally they scratched their heads or rubbed their chins in serious contemplation about their next moves as though their lives depended on it. They were surrounded by a crowd well conversant with the game who was not shy in giving loud advice, to the annoyance or appreciation of the players involved, depending on which side it benefited.

Even though the cafe was closed, people still liked to congregate there. Sitting around the empty table away from the crowded barracks and indulging in idle chat gave them a sense of freedom. This was no real escape from the constant commotion around them, but at least it provided a comforting illusion.

In one of my group's gatherings at the cafe, I learned a frightening fact. Amid all the jokes and noisy banters, suddenly Ban threw me a worried look:

'To think that you had nearly become a pirate's wife, Quynh!'

I didn't know how to react to such a shocking statement as that. Where was that coming from?

'What! Don't you talk nonsense!' I frowned at Ban.

'No, seriously. You had come very close to becoming a pirate's wife.'

What Ban said sounded like a bad joke, but his face told me he was serious.

I had no idea what he was on about.

'Remember the night we were on the trawler?' Ban asked.

'Sure. The fishermen gave us a good meal. Afterwards we and the children sang for them,' I recalled the event cheerfully.

'Well...' Ban hesitated, as though he was not sure whether he should come out and say what was on his mind. 'I think... that trawler might be a pirate ship, and the fishermen on it were pirates,' he gravely surmised.

People in the camp shared their pirate stories and found a common pattern.

In many instances, the pirates pretended to be helpful to the refugees at first. They would allow them to board their boats. The women and the girls would be directed into the cabin, while the men and the boys stayed outside on the open deck. Everyone would be given a meal. When they all felt grateful and dropped their guard, the criminals would attack and rob them. Those who resisted were bashed. Some were even killed and thrown overboard.

Many women, even young girls, were raped. Those who were released back to their boats after the pirates had finished with them counted themselves lucky to be alive, even though 'lucky' could never be the right word to describe their predicament. In many cases, the best looking ones were kidnapped, never to be seen or heard of again.

The first part of this horror story was exactly how things unfolded when my group was allowed to board the trawler. By some random stroke of luck, we had been spared the damning sequence.

Ban said B had found a tiny piece of gold leaf wedged in a tiny crack of the trawler. He had picked it up and had hidden it in his pocket.

Vietnamese and Chinese in South Vietnam preferred to keep their wealth in gold taels or gold leaves. Many carried the family fortune with them in their escapes. They were easy prey for the pirates who waited for them in the open seas, ready to pounce on them.

The broken piece of gold leaf that B had found could have been the result of a fierce and bloody struggle that had taken place on the trawler before the fishermen rescued us. It could have been a silent witness to a tale of horror that had become painfully frequent.

Otherwise, Ban reasoned, what was the likelihood of poor fishermen carrying gold leaves on their fishing trips, carelessly dropping such a valuable piece of metal on their boat?

I recall feeling extremely grateful when my group was allowed to board the trawler. From behind the glass window of their upper floor cabin, I could see the fishermen looking down at us, laughing excitedly among themselves. I was too naïve at the time to give this any dark thought.

I still feel a chill down my spine thinking about what could have happened to me and my female companions the night we were on that trawler over thirty years ago.

After all those years, I still struggle to find an answer to the question—why were we spared?

Could it be because Tam, our steersman, and the trawler owner were both Chinese? Was it thanks to this common bond that the trawler owner decided to show us mercy?

The trawler owner adored Tam's two-year-old daughter. Did her angelic face cause the heart of a criminal to melt? He even asked whether he could adopt her.

We girls had been totally exposed to the elements. Cooped up in the filthy cavity of our tiny boat for days, we were covered in a myriad of grimy substances – sweat, vomit, urine, greasy engine oil. We looked, and smelled, *thankfully*, disgusting. Did this save us?

By the way, human faeces are a *great* way to repel a would-be rapist. Some women described how they scrambled for children's faeces and smeared them all over their face, their body and their clothes the moment a pirate boat approached. That was how they avoided being raped. How I wish that no one – *no one* - has to learn this kind of life lesson.

Could it be that these fishermen just had a good haul from their previous crime spree and we were lucky enough to run into them when they were in their 'down' time?

If they were not pirates, what could possibly be the explanation for that mysterious piece of gold leaf on their trawler?

From accounts of survivors, fishermen from Thailand who were Chinese normally showed compassion and provided assistance to the refugees. Only fishermen who were Thai natives would commit piracy, murder, rape and kidnap on the Vietnamese in such a merciless and inhumane fashion.

According to Vietka (Archives of Vietnamese Boat People):

> *In the 1980s, hundreds of thousands of Vietnamese refugees, while escaping from Vietnam, were massacred in the sea by Thai fishermen turned pirates. The way they killed these refugees, which has been documented, was obnoxiously barbarous, and was certainly far more brutal than that of the Nazis or Pol Pot's clans. In many cases, Thai pirates used hammer, machete, gun to kill the entire boat, including children and women; some were simply dumped to the sea to die slowly.*

Father Joseph Devlin, a Catholic priest who dedicated his life to help the Vietnamese, both during and after the Vietnam War, recalled the harrowing task he faced while in Songkla camp in Thailand:[13]

> *Each morning we would go down to the beaches and there would be bodies—men, women and children—washed ashore during the night. Sometimes there were hundreds of them, like pieces of wood. Some of them were girls who had been raped and then thrown into the sea by pirates to drown. It was tragic beyond words. We would pull them off the beaches and bury them and say prayers for them. This happened every morning. Sometimes I hated to get up in the morning, as the bodies were always there. I wondered if anyone else in the world knew...or cared. Sometimes people would somehow still be alive. They would be on the beach exhausted or unconscious. They washed ashore at night, and we revived them and held them when we found them. They thought we were angels, but we were just men and women who cared.*
>
> *Of course the weather took its toll on the boat people. The boats were terrible. Sometimes the refugees would be caught by Vietnamese authorities and towed back to Vietnam and put in jail. But the pirates were probably the biggest cause of the killing. The pirates stopped nearly every boat. They searched for gold first, even going so far as to take it out of the people's teeth. The next thing that attracted them were the young girls. The pirates were concerned about getting caught, and the best way of not getting caught was to destroy the boat and the people in it and maybe even throw the girls overboard when they were all through with them.*
>
> *Sometimes they passed young girls from boat to boat for 10 days or so, and they were raped hundreds of times. Then sometimes they tied them to ropes and pulled them behind the boats till they were drowned and cut them*

loose. Or they cut their throats and threw them in the sea, or simply just tossed them into the sea. These men were all fishermen, and they kept the girls with them during their work. Then they threw them away like garbage. And then the bodies washed up on shore or just disappeared into the sea.

The State of The World's Refugees 2000: Fifty Years of Humanitarian Action *(Chapter 4 Flight from Indochina)*, a document compiled by the United Nations High Commissioner for Refugees, provides horrific accounts and statistics:

Just in one year, in 1981, among the 452 refugee boats arriving in Thailand with 15,479 people on board, 349 boats were attacked by the pirates, each boat was attacked at least three times, 578 women were raped, 228 women were kidnapped and 881 people were either killed or had disappeared.

UN High Commissioner for Refugees Poul Hartling noted the 'cruelty, brutality and inhumanity that go beyond my imagination.'

The Thai government's action in response to this savagery was vexed. An article titled 'Thai Pirates Preying on Vietnam's refugees' in *The Hour*, Tuesday 26 January 1982, reported:

SONGKLA, THAILAND (Associated Press) – Thai pirates, who last year murdered, raped and abducted hundreds of Vietnamese refugees, continue to have what one observer calls 'an open season on boat people.'

The government of Thailand mounts no special operations against the pirates.

Most international relief officials and Western diplomats dismiss the theory that the Thai government is stalling because it sees the pirates as a deterrent to the unwanted flux of Vietnamese refugees. Privately, however, many foreign officials involved in refugee work say Thai efforts against piracy have been marginal.

There has been little forceful denunciation of the atrocities by the Thai leadership. Instead, official government media have linked the current enmity between Thailand and Vietnam with the refugees fleeing that Communist nation.

A radio station, run by the Thai navy and broadcasting in southern Thailand, recently noted that the entry of Vietnamese refugees constituted 'a national security burden' and warned that Thai fishermen who helped the refugees were 'damaging our security'.

'The pirates half think that they are doing their country a favour. It's a good way of salving their conscience,' says a relief worker who interviewed hundreds of piracy victims.

The UNHCR has praised the Thai legal system once pirate subjects are brought before a court and noted that this year, 23 Thais were charged in eight separate, piracy-related cases. 'But getting witnesses to testify is the tough part. They'd be dead within a week for starters,' one UNHCR official says.

The refugees invariably were forewarned about pirates, either from foreign radio broadcasts or letters sent by relatives abroad.

'A lot of them seem to regard it as a necessary evil and take the experience with remarkable stoicism, especially the women. They are real heroines in my book,' says Rev. Joseph Devlin, a Roman Catholic priest who works with refugees here.

After all this time, my feelings about this period of my life are still a tangled mess of contrasting and confounding emotions. Survivors of tragedies often experience guilt. I know it is part of my psyche. I am grateful for having been given a new chance in life. At the same time, I feel infinitely sad for those who did not make it. My excitement at just being alive, of waking up and seeing the sunrise at the break of dawn, is dampened by a profound sense of powerlessness and unworthiness. I vacillate between calm acceptance about a situation that was beyond my control and angry indignation at the calamities that befell the innocent men, women and children of my nation.

Dr. Viktor Frankl wrote:[14]

> *When a man finds that it is his destiny to suffer, he will have to accept his suffering as his task... [a task] to get through... The way in which a man accepts his fate and all the suffering it entails, the way in which he takes up his cross, gives him ample opportunity – even under the most difficult circumstances – to add a deeper meaning to his life... Here lies the chance for a man either to make use or to forego the opportunities of attaining the moral values that a difficult situation may afford him. And this decides whether he is worthy of his sufferings or not.*

There was nothing that I could do, that anyone could do, to change the script life had written, damnably, for us, victims of a particularly wicked brand of dictatorship—the Vietnamese Communist dictatorship.

We can't control our destiny, but hopefully we can overcome it.

Hopefully we are worthy of our sufferings.

Those of us who survived are no more deserving than those who had perished, but we had been given the chance to live in freedom and they had not. Hopefully we do not take our survival for granted and know how to use our freedom in a meaningful way.

My stepsister My and my sister Ba must have understood what the boys left unsaid about our encounter with the fishermen, but they did not explain it to me.

This was the late seventies. I was eighteen at the time. Like all young Vietnamese women of conservative and traditional upbringing, I was totally ignorant about sex. In that small town of mine, sex was something that happened behind closed doors. Children of my generation were not bombarded with sex from various mediums as in Western countries today, even though this trend seemed to be catching up in Asian societies.

I was familiar with Vietnamese, Chinese and French classics, I read Dostoevsky translated into Vietnamese, yet I did not know *exactly* how a baby was made. Neither did my girlfriends. At eighteen we still speculated among ourselves that by sitting on a chair a man had just sat on, a woman could get herself pregnant!

Sex was not publicly mentioned or talked about. Young brides of traditional upbringing would discover how babies were made on their wedding night. Married women shared that secret among themselves and never revealed it to the uninitiated.

In classic literary masterpieces, lovers exchanged tender looks and poetry. In modern romantic novels, they held hands and planted light kisses on the cheek. Why mention sexual intercourse by its name when ambiguous metaphors, such as 'making the clouds and the rain', or 'making the moon and the flowers', could perfectly convey the same meaning?

Nothing prepared me for the violent world. No one mentioned the word 'rape'. In the camp no one mentioned *that* word either. People used the vague term 'subject to *it*', or left a blank for you to fill, followed by a heavy, painful silence.

When my group first arrived at the camp, an elderly lady approached and asked me in an extremely concerned voice, 'Were you...?' I had not quite understood what she implied.

I felt annoyed at Ban. How dare he say I had nearly become a pirate's wife! What silly nonsense!

The Beauty That Remains

The mounting human backlog in the Southeast Asian refugee camps had forced the United Nations High Commissioner for Refugees to process people's applications for permanent settlement with greater urgency.

In my camp the names of those leaving for third countries were announced through the PA sytem more frequently. Groups of newcomers would fill their places almost immediately. This new flow of refugees consisted mainly of young men and women of 'tainted' background who escaped to avoid being sent to the battlefield in Cambodia.

***

Territorial skirmishes between Cambodia and Vietnam started soon after the Khmer Rouge took power in Cambodia in 1975 and escalated into an all-out war in 1978.

Children of former South Vietnamese government personnel, outcasts in their own society, became favourite targets of the 'volunteer' recruitment drives. 'Volunteers' would be sent to the battlefields as cannon fodder or war coolies.

Perversely, this was a cruel chance for these young men and women to gain acceptance from a system that had rejected them so emphatically. The Party's secretary Vo Van Kiet was the driving force behind the 'volunteer labour units' program in the Saigon-Gia Dinh area. In his talk to the first crop of volunteers at the Thong Nhat (Reunification) sports oval in the morning of 28 March 1976, Kiet addressed the much despised 'children of the lackeys' as 'my beloved little brothers and sisters'. This was the first time these kids were addressed in such affectionate terms by a Party high-up. The journalist and historian Huy Duc wrote that Kiet's speech brought many of them to tears.[15]

Kiet was painted as a more humane member of the inhumane Party machine. And yet, his humane touch could be seen as a poisoned chalice, a well-choreographed sinister ploy even. He had opened a door of hope to a group of desperate youngsters; that door was hard labour and death. The tears they shed might not be tears of appreciation for having finally been included in society, as Huy Duc seemed to convey, but tears of dejection and bitterness for being pushed to a deadly corner, again, albeit with nicer sounding rhetoric this time round.

Against the ruthless Khmer Rouge, these city kids had not been given any battle training, not even for one day.[16] They were tasked with tending and carrying the injured, burying the dead, transporting ammunition, building roads, clearing heavily muddy paths by filling them with dirt or tree bark for troops to pass.[17] Their work could be even harder and more harrowing than engaging in battles.

More perversely, although they were thrown into the line of fire, they were still not trusted. At the beginning, most of them were not even armed. Many died horrific deaths. On 22 July 1978, a Vietnamese platoon of 'volunteers', Platoon 3, which included an all-female squad, encountered a Khmer Rouge unit. Of the fifty members of the platoon, only two carried weapons. They were lambs to the slaughter. A massacre ensued. Only two of them survived. Seven female 'volunteers' were raped before being brutally killed.[18] Even after these deaths, according to Vo Viet Thanh, a captain of the People's Army in charge of volunteer units in the Saigon-Gia Dinh area, many Party leaders maintained their open disdain towards South Vietnamese 'volunteers' and barked at anyone who questioned the glaringly unconscionable policy of sending these youngsters into harm's way without arming them:[19]

'Providing weapons to this motley group of unreliable family background, are you out of your mind?'

'If for some reason this rag-tag mob disbanded, no one could foresee the consequence.'

Vo Van Kiet was the one who fought for their right to arm.[20]

On 7 January 1979, Ho Ngoc Dai, the Party General Secretary Le Duan's son-in-law, woke him up from a midday nap to inform him of important news.

'Our troops have entered Cambodia's capital, Phnom Penh,' Dai said.

'Uh-huh,' Duan mumbled, then went back to his nap.

'I was shocked... I could not believe that he could just fall back to sleep after such earth-shattering news,' Dai said.

To bring a great army to invade another's nation's capital seemed easy and peaceful, like an emperor's nap, yet it took the Vietnamese army ten years to pull out of Cambodia, Huy Duc wrote.[21]

Following its military victory, Vietnam set up a puppet regime in Cambodia. Vietnam saw its presence in Cambodia in a noble light: to save the Cambodian people from Khmer Rouge butchery. Its neighbors and the international community saw it as an invasion. China was neither happy with its former protégé's hegemonic ambition nor Vietnam's close ties with the Soviet Union. It switched support to the Khmer Rouge and abandoned its promise to provide aid to help build post-war Vietnam.

For the next ten years, Vietnam was shunned by China, isolated by its neighbours, and punished with economic sanctions by the international community.

Internally, ideology-driven policies had destroyed the formerly vibrant South Vietnamese economy. Mass nationalisation brought business and industry activities to a halt. Following a money exchange operation, each household was only allowed a maximum of 200 *revolutionary dong*, the equivalent of 400 kilograms of rice at official price - the new limit to a family's wealth. Food became a scarcity.[22] The military adventure and the burden of maintaining a puppet regime in Cambodia had squandered immense resources that could have been used towards the rebuilding of post-war Vietnam. Topping these problems with international economic sanctions, Vietnam in peacetime was plunged into unprecedented poverty and misery. Hundreds of thousands of 'volunteers', in both combat and non-combat roles, were either killed or maimed in the war with the Khmer Rouge in Cambodia.[23] The Communist 'emperor' Le Duan's peaceful nap cost his country that much.

***

Xuan, my sister Ba's friend, was the first person in my group to leave Kota Bharu camp. She possessed an agreeable profile: single, university educated and having a relative in France who was happy to sponsor her. Those with a similar profile would have no trouble getting a nod from the immigration officers of various countries. Unskilled people with young children tended to be picked last.

Xuan's relative sent her a cheque of US$100 so she could buy nice clothes to wear on the plane, in order to make a good impression on the people of her adopted country. She gave that cheque to my family. She was heading to a new life in France, while we would never know for sure how much longer we would remain in the camp. We were deeply moved by her generosity.

Xuan's father was a high level Cao Dai priest who had been locked up in a Communist prison.

Thanks to Xuan's cheque, my family and our good friends Ban and Vu could have a taste of the good life again. That meant plenty of bread, milk, instant noodles, Ovaltine, and an absolutely wonderful thing that I had not seen for a very long time—*milk biscuits*!

The kiosk was allowed to reopen. The camp's authority could see the trading ban had not only hurt the refugees, but the local economy as well. The food trucks were allowed back into the camp and transformed its front yard into a lively market again.

On 30 December 1978 my family received good news. Our names were on the next departure list. We would leave the camp on 27 January 1979, almost three months to the day since we set foot on the Malaysian shore.

This was the news I had been waiting for, yet I could not help feeling sad at having to say farewell to Ban and Vu. Like grains of dust, we would soon scatter in four directions. Would we ever meet again?

Soon after she heard of my family's impending departure, A came to see me at my sleep site. Since the break-up of my group into the 'haves' and 'have-nots', A and I had not been on speaking terms. I was not sure what to expect.

Perhaps she came to say good-bye. Perhaps she was being *nice* at last. 'Perhaps we can be friends again,' I thought to myself.

'I want my shirt back. Give it to me,' A said.

I was taken aback by her cold and abrupt manner.

'What...what shirt??' I asked.

I had more than enough hand-me-downs. There was no need for me to borrow anything from her or from anybody else.

'The shirt that the officer from the Thai Navy gave me,' A said.

I was astounded.

The Thai Navy officer gave it to me and not to her. It had been with me ever since, literally even when I slept. I had bundled it with other pieces of clothing to make myself a makeshift pillow.

'Liar,' I thought to myself, feeling quite indignant.

I should have confronted her. I should have told her off.

Instead, I quietly unfolded my makeshift pillow, took the shirt out and handed it to her. She snatched it and walked away.

I had never been in a situation where I had to fight over anything. After all, it was only a shirt. Nice people don't fight over a shirt, do they?

Those on the departure list excitedly prepared for the big day. They would spread what little possessions they had on their sites, musing on what to keep and what to give away to their neighbours. Simple things that might not amount to much in normal circumstances, such as mosquito nets, blankets, buckets, spoons and eating bowls, were precious in this place.

Those with money were even allowed to go to town, accompanied by a Malaysian officer, for a shopping spree. They would come back with bags of nice clothes and nice shoes. Everyone wanted to go to their new homeland looking their best.

These people would gush about their trips to the outside world to an appreciative and envious audience. For those whose flight to a new land was still a fair wait away, their world did not go beyond this fenced enclosure in the middle of nowhere.

'The Malaysian shopping centre is so beautiful!' a lady exclaimed. 'You can even try on the clothes before buying!'

I felt excited just to listen to her.

In Hollywood movies, travelling by plane always seemed like a glamorous occasion. Flight passengers tended to dress up for the trip. I would love to have nice clothes to wear on the plane too, but Xuan's gift of US$100 could only stretch so far.

To prepare for my family's trip to Australia, my sister Ba went to the kiosk to buy perfumed soap and toilet paper – in case there was no perfumed soap or toilet paper in Australia! Not knowing much about this mysterious country, we might as well prepare for the worst!

Ba also bought a cheap suitcase to put these in, together with the odd pieces of clothing that we had accumulated. I dismantled a dress to make a cloth bag for my most cherished possessions – my songbook and my diary.

27 January 1979 (Lunar New Year's Eve)
The day my family would say goodbye to Kota Bharu camp had arrived. We got up early to get ourselves ready. Linh

folded the mosquito net and the blanket and placed them neatly on a corner of the plank. These were for our successors.

I had been counting the days to this moment. Now that my earnest wish had become a reality, my feeling of excitement had been replaced by solemn reflection. I sensed the importance of the day—like the silent working of destiny.

The rest of the barracks were still soundly asleep. I could hear their quiet breathing inside the mosquito nets. It was hard to imagine this serene atmosphere would descend into hurly-burly in a few hours' time.

Outside, the first rays of sunlight had appeared. The gentle morning breeze whiffled through the windows, reeking of sewage.

An ambulance came to fetch us. We said farewell to Ban and Vu and set off for Kuala Lumpur.

The ambulance dropped us off at a bus depot. I held onto the shiny handrail attached to the bus door to climb on it and eased myself into the velvet cushioned seat, feeling overwhelmed with joy.

Three long years living in acute deprivation and regressing to backwardness under the Communists, plus three months living under the most basic of conditions in the refugee camp, had turned this simple bus ride into a sensational experience for me.

We didn't just climb onto a bus. We climbed back to civilisation!

I took in a deep breath. The clean, fresh air travelled to my lungs, rejuvenating every cell in my body; my tongue could even taste its sweetness. I observed all the luxuries in the bus with intense amusement. The air-conditioning, the soft music coming out from the speakers, the lace curtain at every window. There was even a flush toilet at the back of the bus!

My face stayed glued to the bus window. The enchanting and graceful Malaysian scenery gradually revealed itself. We travelled past quiet country towns with wide boulevards and pretty wooden houses painted in bright colours, the typical Malaysian way. We stopped for lunch at a roadside stall and reached the outskirts of Kuala Lumpur that night.

The bus went by sleepy streets and imposing villas before entering the commercial district. My eyes opened wide with admiration: splendidly lit and impossibly tall buildings, flashing billboards, multicoloured shop signs, huge supermarkets, numerous beautiful shop fronts displaying the latest fashion. People in smart clothes sat inside elegant restaurants with stark white tablecloths.

An inviting picture of modernity, affluence and enjoyment. These were the things the Vietnamese people had missed out on since the dark days of the Communist takeover.

The bus rolled into an underground depot and parked next to a Red Crescent van. The Red Cross operates as the Red Crescent in Muslim countries. As we alighted from the bus, a young man of European appearance got out of the van and walked towards us.

'Hello! My name is Larry. I'm from the Red Crescent. How are you?'

Larry brought us to an eating place nearby and ordered *curry mee* for everyone. He was from Portugal. The rescue mission of Vietnamese refugees had truly been an international effort.

After the meal, Larry bought a string of Chinese firecrackers and a box of matches, then gave them to my brother.

'Tonight is New Year's Eve for Vietnamese and Chinese, isn't it?' he smiled.

I was touched by his kindness.

Tin struck a match. We jumped back as the firecrackers exploded. Shreds of paper petards scattered on the ground like red confetti, the colour of happiness. We broke out laughing.

Larry drove us in the Red Crescent van to a transit camp called Cheras. Upon their arrival in Kuala Lumpur, refugees were brought to different transit camps where they would

The Beauty That Remains

stay and wait for their flights to their new homeland. Those destined for Australia stayed in Belfield camp, while those going to America and Canada stayed in Cheras camp. We were supposed to stay in Belfield camp, however because it was currently overcrowded, we were sent to Cheras instead.

Cheras camp was within the precinct of a church. The refugees were housed in the main church building and in tents erected on an empty land area adjacent to it. The camp was in celebratory mode when we arrived.

'Dear compatriots, we warmly invite you all to come out to the front yard to welcome the Lunar New Year!' a happy male voice announced from the loudspeaker.

A strong smell - a headachy mixture of the stench of sewage, rubbish, and the fragrance of burning incense sticks - hung thick in the air. Vietnamese and Chinese burn incense sticks in all important traditional ceremonies.

Behind a tall chicken wire fence, in the camp's dimly lit and narrow front yard, a packed crowd was waiting to celebrate the new year.

One of the camp coordinators unlocked the gate to let us in. He smiled warmly to us. That was the only formality. We were then left to our own devices. We pushed our way into the building against a stream of people who were pouring out towards the front yard.

Inside, the atmosphere was pleasantly quiet, at least until the assembling crowd outside returned. The high vaulted ceiling and a large cross on the wall in the sanctuary reminded everyone that this shelter used to be a place of worship. The serene presence of the cross and the message of love and compassion it represented gave me an immediate sense of comfort. There were people who fled Vietnam with just the clothes on their backs and a cross in their hands or a gold chain with a small Buddha pendant around their necks for divine protection.

The soft light emitted from the fluorescent tubes on the high ceiling lent this place a warm, spacious feel. Those who chose to stay in were either sitting up or lying down at their sites, keeping to themselves. The sacred time when the clock struck midnight was approaching. Everyone seemed to be in a contemplative mood.

People's possessions, including their bags, their buckets, blankets, slippers and eating utensils, were arranged in a straight line between sleep sites. They formed a kind of makeshift fence to mark personal territories.

We struggled to find a vacant place.

A lean-to was attached to this main building. A row of bunk beds was installed along its length, leaving just enough space for a narrow walkway leading to the camp kitchen. All the beds were occupied.

The walkway seemed to be the last in-door spot that had not been taken. We put our bags down. This would be our place.

I rested my back against the wall. The concrete floor was cold and the wall was hard, but at least we did not have to sleep under the open sky.

People tripped over my feet as they filed past. I bent my knees to make room for them.

'Do you want to go out to celebrate the New Year?' my little sister Linh asked.

I shook my head in exhaustion. I just wanted to lie down, but would have to wait for the gathering to end and for people to go back to their places before I could get any peace.

Whiffs of sewage came out from under a crack on the floor near my feet. I would have to put up with this putrid smell this night and many nights to come. The thought filled me with resignation.

The loud clattering of firecrackers from the front yard had stopped. The happy voice from the loudspeaker changed to mournful:

'Please observe one minute of silence to commemorate our friends, our loved ones and our compatriots who unfortunately have perished at sea on their journeys in search of freedom.

Let's also remember those who are languishing in the re-education camps and those who still suffer under Communist tyranny in our prayers. Let's pray that freedom, one day, will return to our beloved motherland.'

A popular New Year song came out from the loudspeaker. The familiar and happy tune brought a smile to the many faces still haunted by fresh tragedies.

My diary entry:

> *Dear Mother and Father,*
>
> *It's Lunar New Year Eve and I wonder what you are doing right now, at this very moment? Mother, do you still place nice offerings on the altar for Buddha and our ancestors? Or are you too sad to perform these rituals because all your children are away, somewhere unknown, and you don't even know whether they are already dead or still alive.*
>
> *I miss you most, Mother. I miss our blue house, the blue gate, the blue garage door, the blue window frames. Blue must be Father's favourite colour. He painted everything in blue, perhaps to match the colour of the sky. I miss the green garden that glows under the bright midday sun. I miss my woollen blanket and the warm bed. I miss the uneventfulness of everyday. I now know that a day that is as predictable as the day before and the day after is a blessing. I remember a time when everything was running like clockwork - wake up, go to school, back from school, have lunch, have a siesta, have dinner, do homework, then go to sleep. It is always cold in that mountain city of ours. Yet, tonight, as I'm sitting on the hard concrete floor in a strange place in a strange country, my memory is of a warm place and cosy nights.*
>
> *Dear Mother, every night you would come to the girls' bedroom to keep us company. You would sit next to us*

and knit while we were doing our homework. It was pitch dark outside, it might even be rainy and windy as it often is in our city; but inside, everything was nice and quiet. You waited for Linh and me to finish homework and snuggle nicely in bed, before switching off the light and gently closed the door behind you. The world was as safe as your smile when you bid us goodnight. Nothing could go wrong. Wasn't it, Mother? There was a time when nothing could go wrong.

***

'Have your group registered your names with the kitchen staff?' A young man from the upper level of the bunk bed opposite where I sat moved closer to the edge of the bed and looked down at me. 'You'd better do it now, otherwise you'll have no food tomorrow,' he said.

I thanked him for the helpful tip. I noticed that he was paralysed from the waist down. He had to use his arms to lift his body up and drag it from one end of the bed to the other end with difficulty. I wondered whether he was handicapped from birth or the pirates had broken his legs. During the escape, some men were bashed, maimed or killed by the pirates because they had tried to fight back, or because they had tried to protect the women from being raped.

There was a food queue in the morning for breakfast and another one at midday for the main meal. As dinner was not provided, the kitchen staff gave out generous servings at these times, so people had enough food to sustain them for the rest of the day. At breakfast each person was given several slices of bread, a thick slab of butter, a big scoop of sugar and plenty of milk. For the main meal, there was always cooked rice accompanied by a meat dish, a vegetable dish, and one boiled egg for each person every day. The meat dish and the vegetable dish changed daily.

Compared with the unchanged diet of rice and tinned sardines in Kota Bharu camp, this was a restaurant menu to me. Compared with the starving Communist ration, this was unimaginable luxury. And yet, for some strange reason, I experienced a sudden loss of appetite. I wondered if this had something to do with my newly found spirituality. My reduced interest in food—a rare and welcome occurrence because it had helped me shed some unwanted weight—happened to coincide with my recent passion to go to church.

My family was not Catholic, but I always loved listening to hymns. These ethereal sounds seemed to possess a special power that could bring instant comfort to my heart. South Vietnam, the society I grew up in, espoused religious freedom. My classmates and I learned to be respectful and open-minded about other people's religions. Whether of Catholic or Buddhist faith, during Lunar New Year festival we all went to the temple to pray to Buddha and check our fortune. We exchanged beautiful Christmas cards with each other at Christmas. I liked to think Jesus and Buddha were brothers.

Every afternoon, refugees who were Catholic were allowed to leave the camp to attend mass. My sisters, my stepsister and I would join them. We talked with other churchgoers and discovered that some of them were also unconfirmed believers like us. Since God was all-loving, I was sure he did not mind whether we had been baptised or not, and would care for each and every single human being all the same.

My brother, on the other hand, suspected the girls harboured worldly motives in flocking to church. Among the churchgoers were members of a pop group that was quite famous in South Vietnam before the Communist takeover.

Of course I protested my pure intention, but not too vehemently, as I did have my eyes on the tallest and most charming among them. Perhaps this was the real reason for my sudden desire to go on a diet. When Linh commented on my slender figure, I did not say anything, but felt quietly happy. Hopefully the 'object of my interest' also noticed this.

'Here come the shameless self-promoters!' Tin said when he saw we girls combing our hair and checking ourselves in the mirror before going to mass. We could be sharp-tongued when the situation called for it, however this time we giggled instead of retorting, which could be construed—rightly—by him as an admission of guilt.

The fact that the local church provided its main hall to shelter the refugees, no matter what religion they belonged to, said more about Christianity than the most powerful sermon. Mass was now held in an open chapel built on a small hill next to the camp, a simple but gracious wooden structure that sat high on a wide stone staircase.

The local men, women and children all looked stunning in their smart church outfits. I felt embarrassed to stand next to them. My clothes were some odds and ends from charity, my footwear a shabby pair of thongs. I felt depressed at our glaring disparity. These people seemed at ease with themselves and their surroundings: they possessed poise and confidence; they knew their place in the world; they were part of *normal* society. As for me, a refugee, I felt as though I needed an excuse for my existence. I thought of a time when I was like them.

As if wanting to dispel my concerns, a young family came to sit next to me. The father greeted me with a courteous nod, the mother gave me a warm smile, and at her prodding, their adorable young daughter shyly extended her hand to me. They might not know how much these kindly gestures meant to me.

After mass, with the beautiful hymns still resonating in my ears, I would descend the steep stairs to go back to the camp, back to my quarantined existence behind high fence and locked gate, but the thought there was a higher being who kept watch over me, and nice people who treated me with kindness, filled me with happiness.

The crowd, the queues, and the hard concrete floor no longer bothered me as much as they did before. There was a nice shift in my mentality. I came to realise that there existed so many wonderful things in life that I should be thankful for.

My diary entry:

> 1 February 1979
>
> *One learns to get used to one's circumstances. Having experienced so much hardship, I've found that I can endure anything. Happiness seems to come from learning to accept things that I can't change and stop being demanding.*
>
> *There is so much beauty in this place: the blue sky, the green forest, the stone staircase, the chapel, the beautiful hymns. I feel happy.*

Linh's diary entry, written in French:

> 7 February 1979
>
> *Une troupe d'ecoliers visite l'eglise. Ca me rappelle de mon ecole, de mes amis, de mes chers professeurs. Quand puis-je aller a l'ecole avec des amis, avec une cartable ? Je verrai le grand tableau noir et les mots ecrits en craies blancs. Je trouverai un bon professeur qui sera mon bon conseiller comme Mr X. Je jouerai avec les amis de memes ages, de memes pensees comme moi.*
>
> *A group of students comes to the church. They remind me of my school, my friends and my dear teachers. When will I get to go back to school with my friends, carrying my school bag again? I will get to see writing in white chalk on the blackboard again. I will find a good teacher who is also a good counsellor, like my old teacher Mr X. I will get to play with friends my age who think like me.*

A Vietnamese priest asked me, my stepsister and my sisters whether we would like to join the church choir. Given our regular attendance at mass, there was no reason for him to doubt whether we were true devotees or not. We, in turn, did not think there was any need to clarify this. My brother again reprimanded us for joining the choir under false pretense, however I believed our sincerity was sufficient.

Adjacent to the chapel on top of the stone staircase was the monastery. Every night, the choir members were allowed to go there to rehearse. The Malaysian priests were exceptionally kind to us. They brought out tea and sweets on a tray, placed censers around the rehearsal room to ward off the mosquitoes, then sat in armchairs to relax and enjoy our singing.

They reminded me of my French teacher, Sister Catherine, a Catholic nun. The last time I saw her was when I rode my bike to Nazareth Convent to visit her, at the news that the Communist authorities had placed all the nuns at the convent under house arrest. So many things had happened to me since, as though I had lived many lives.

The sparse forest surrounding the monastery bore poignant resemblance to my hometown. The landscape was both touchingly familiar and palpably remote. I suddenly realised the innocent world I used to inhabit, the world of a normal teenager whose life simply revolved around her family and her school friends, who had never experienced anything more tragic than the death of her cat or her pet rabbit, had truly vanished. It only reappeared, like now, in unprompted, sudden bouts of reminiscence, catching me off guard, leaving me reeling with a profound sadness bordering on grief.

Every day hundreds of people were brought to this transit camp by bus. They filled the places of hundreds of others who had just left for a new life. In this state of flux, it might have been thought wise not to form any close emotional bond, and yet I made many new friends here. Our friendships were intense. In our vulnerability, we felt much closer to one another. We shared confidences and stories of our lives unreservedly, perhaps because this was the last place where our past and our present still retained its full significance. Understanding and compassion often proved more healing than spoken words, helped complete unfinished sentences, mend broken souls and give solace to painful silence.

Soon we would be scattered in different corners of the globe, where our history, our culture, our sufferings, our tragic journey, what we had known and been familiar with all our lives would be irrelevant, as though they had never existed. In a sense, we had all died and were now heading to our next reincarnation. We would all have to start our lives on a clean slate, forge a new identity, learn to think, act and speak again—like an infant.

After three weeks in Cheras, my family was transported to a Red Crescent centre in Belfield, where refugees destined for Australia stayed waiting for their flights. An Australian lady gave us a crash course about our new homeland. Perhaps she was under the assumption that we already possessed some basic knowledge about Australia—who didn't, really!—and so did not think it was necessary to show us pictures of big towns, big cities, high-rise buildings and crowded markets. For developed nations such as Australia, these would be considered commonplace. Instead, she showed us photos of people and animals that were unique to Australia: Aborigines in the outback and native animals, such as kangaroos, koalas and wombats, in a landscape of dry desert land and lone eucalyptus trees. As a result, Australia as I pictured it in my mind was a vastly under-populated country—this would turn out to be true—possibly not as modern and developed as France or America—this would turn out to be absolutely incorrect—and a large part of Australian land was still wilderness—that was a good guess.

I was fascinated by the kangaroo. A large animal that could stand on its two hind legs and had a bag in front of its stomach to carry its baby around, the way Asian mothers tug their babies in their mei-tais. It seemed so magical that I almost half-expected it could also talk like Walt Disney's cartoon animal characters!

The following afternoon we boarded a Boeing 747 heading for Melbourne.

I had never been in a plane, let alone this gigantic flying machine. I had never heard of Melbourne. I wondered what this city had in store for me.

I could not contain my excitement. Just being seated inside this wonder of technology was a joy for me. The noise and the heat of the refugee camp were nicely replaced with the quiet comfort of the air-conditioned cabin. The tall blond stewardesses all looked beautiful and glamorous like the femme fatales in Hollywood movies. Ba, Linh and I were seated next to each other. We took turns to occupy the coveted window seat. I had a bit of a fright and my ears hurt badly when the plane took off, but afterwards I was amply compensated with the wonderful bird's-eye view of earth landscapes below: cities that banded together like a gigantic mosaic, nature's harmonious colour schemes of green fields, brown earth and meandering blue rivers that were simply picture-perfect.

'We are as high as the clouds! Can you believe it!' Linh shook her head in disbelief.

We were literally on cloud nine, and when I was served tea and coffee by these movie stars in Qantas uniforms, who were so gracious and courteous even to refugees like me, I also believed in angels!

The Beauty That Remains

My camp vaccination booklet (1978)

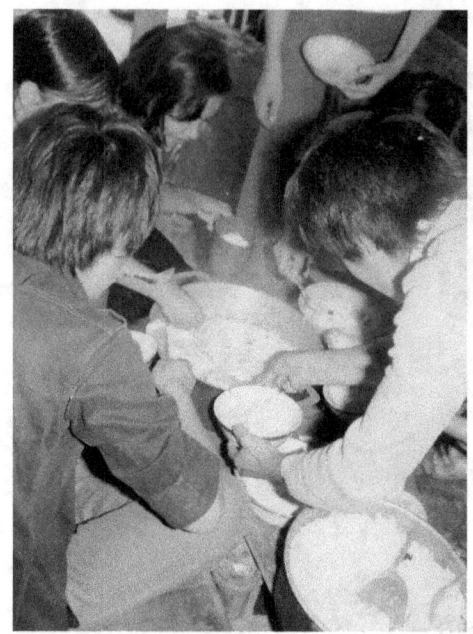

Lunch with rice and instant noodles soup at Kota Bharu camp (1978)

Queuing at the camp water pump: my niece holds a bucket, her dad stands behind (1978)

The Beauty That Remains

With our friends at Kota Bharu camp, some are enjoying Coke in plastic bags bought from the camp kiosk behind us (1979) Standing left to right: little sister Linh, sister Ba, Quynh, stepsister My, brother Chau and our niece, a friend, stepbrother Tuan. Sitting down: brother Tin (third from left).

Linh's camp diary written in French

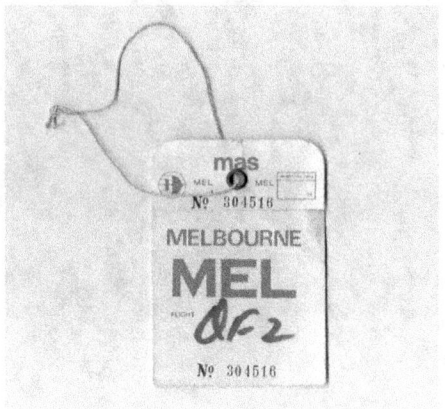

My family's Qantas luggage tag
and my boarding pass to Australia,
our new homeland (1979)

PART III

THE LAND OF SUNSHINE

19 February 1979
It was a beautiful summer's day when we arrived at Tullamarine Airport outside Melbourne.

We got off the plane and were led into the airport complex. I had never seen a building so vast. I craned my neck to look at the soaring ceiling. Everything was so bright; everything seemed to sparkle. Through the huge floor-to-ceiling glass panels, I could see hundreds of cars of different sizes and colours in the car park outside. I had never seen so many cars before; for a moment I thought they were toy cars. Everybody dressed nicely and walked with quick, confident steps.

The transition was so fast. A part of me was still wondering whether the world dogged by mischance and uncertainty on the other side of the sea was truly behind me. I walked my first steps into this new world of sunshine and space tentatively, timidly, full of wonder, as though I were walking into a dream.

A bus drove us along wide and well-paved streets, past quiet suburbs with similar looking single-storey houses. Occasionally a high-rise appeared in the distance, towering over low roof tops, grey and awkward, perhaps an inadvertent mistake in this carefully designed landscape. The trees stood equidistant from each other, like a line of well-trained soldiers. There was no rubbish in the streets. Everything seemed to be where it should be. Already I was impressed at Australia's orderliness.

A vague concern troubled me.

How am I going to fit into this perfect order?

The bus entered a service road leading to a large multi-apartment complex. We were dropped off in front of the reception area. Another group of passengers from another bus had also just alighted. They were all Europeans. We and the Europeans were then ushered into an assembly hall.

An Asian lady with a cheerful face and a friendly manner said something in English, then to my absolute delight, in perfect Vietnamese:

'Welcome to Australia. Welcome to Midway Hostel.'

A Vietnamese-speaking person in this foreign land? Her few words had lifted a huge weight off my heart. It was as though I had just landed on the Moon and were greeted by its inhabitants in Earth language.

I was more than impressed when she told us that she came from Laos and spoke five languages fluently. She was the hostel's interpreter.

She gave the newcomers a brief introduction about Australia. It was the only country in the world that occupied a whole continent; its people came from many parts of the world. The most important thing she wanted us to remember was that Australians were very punctual. She said she needed to emphasise this point, especially to we Vietnamese, because from her experience with other Vietnamese, they tended not to be on time.

'For Australians, time is money; one o'clock means one o'clock,' she said.

She was right. For Vietnamese, one o'clock meant… when you were ready. This lack of concern about time and punctuality might have stemmed from the Buddhist belief in reincarnation. When one has many lives to live, time is infinite; there is no need to get all stressed out about time in the present. This bad cultural trait could also be a remnant of an ancient civilisation of nearly 5000 years. For our ancestors, who lived in a simple and innocent pre-modern world, their village was their universe. Nothing earth-shattering could happen there, life stayed more or less the same for millennia. Why the rush?

After her brief talk, the interpreter gave each family a key to their *flat*. She explained 'flat' was the Australian term for 'apartment'. She reminded us about meal times and off we went—to our new lives.

I had been used to omnipresent, obnoxious and illiterate Communist bureaucrats who jumped at every chance to flaunt their importance and give lengthy homilies whenever there was a gathering. So I was surprised when there were no overbearing Australian officials in sight, keen on being at the centre of attention and standing before everyone to deliver their speeches.

This was my first insight into the way Australians operated: efficient, to the point, with minimum fuss and no unnecessary formality. I liked it already.

The four of us—my brother Tin, my older sister Ba, my little sister Linh and I—were given a four-room flat on the first floor of an apartment block. My brother Chau, his wife and their young daughter were allocated another flat in a different block. My stepbrother Tuan stayed with friends. My stepsister My had been scheduled for another flight. She would join us several months later.

I could not believe the four of us had this four-room flat all to ourselves! We shared one bathroom and one toilet. I had my own room and my own bed. This was unimaginable luxury!

I stepped gingerly on the clean, vinyl floor surface, not wanting to soil it with my shoes. Then I took off the shoes and threw myself on the soft mattress, rolled around a few times in pure delight, pressed my nose against the bed sheet and took in a few deep breaths. The beautiful smell of clean linen brought me back to the sunny days of my childhood, when Mother took advantage of the nice weather to wash the clothes and the bed sheets, then hung them on the lines in the garden to let them dry in the sun. Linh and I would swirl in and out of the drooping bed sheets, inhaling that joy-filled concoction of fresh air, crisp sun, and the sweet-scented breeze that carried the smell of all the fruits in season in Mother's orchard, tinged with the faint odour of washing detergent trapped in them.

Outside the window of my room, the glowing Australian sunlight could not wait to be invited in. I stood up, went to the window and opened it. The warm afternoon breeze came flooding in. This was heaven!

We left our bags on the floor and went outside to explore.

This huge complex spread over an extensive area of flat land dotted with tall eucalyptus trees and interspersed with small, well tended gardens. Our block of flats was among many identical-looking ones, with single, sloped roofs and grey-brownish walls. Beautifully mowed lawn and bright green hedges bordered the concrete walkway linking different areas of the hostel with each other. My new surroundings were a world away from the noise and the crowd of a refugee camp. With relish I anticipated quiet strolls in this peaceful setting.

For now we were too timid to venture far. We went back to the car park in front of the assembly hall and stood around, hoping to talk to someone to find out more about this place.

Having lived under a repressive regime, I had been conditioned to think that I was not allowed to do anything unless and until the authorities gave me permission. As we were standing in the empty car park, I could not help feeling a bit nervous. I half-expected someone would come wagging his finger, telling us off. We had not exactly been told we could gather here.

Two Asian men came out from the grocery store adjacent to the assembly hall. We were not sure whether they were Vietnamese or not until they approached and talked to us.

These refugees had been totally transformed. I looked at their glowing skin and shiny hair with envy. They looked quite smart in the typical Western casual outfit of printed T-shirts, blue jeans and sneakers.

From the way they looked at us and at the clothes we were wearing, I could sense they felt a bit sorry for us.

'There's a Sunday market near here that sells very good second-hand clothes at very cheap prices,' one man said.

'But we don't have any money!' I thought to myself.

'The government here is not like the Communists. It gives money to poor people. You will get a government allowance and can spend on whatever you want,' the other man added.

As though he could read my mind!

'I can even save up to send gifts to my relatives in Vietnam!' he boasted.

This sounded so reassuring.

He handed my brother a five-dollar note.

'My gift to you all. Please take it,' he said.

My brother thanked him, went straight into the grocery store and came out with a bunch of grapes, one bottle of Coke and one bottle of Fanta for us to share. It had been years since I last tasted them.

Late that afternoon we had our first meal at the hostel's canteen. I had never been to a restaurant before, let alone an eating place *this* big.

Back in Dalat, my home town, eating in restaurants was a luxury. Two Chinese restaurants in the main business district mainly catered for wedding receptions. Hawkers' stalls were a more popular and affordable option. People sat slurping beef noodle soup on wooden benches or tiny stools placed on footpaths.

The hostel canteen only catered for its residents: refugees from Indo-China—this group consisted of Vietnamese, Laotians and Cambodians; new migrants from Europe; a small number of Australian students from the countryside who came to the city to study and chose to stay at this budget place to save money.

I joined the long queue at the canteen. I observed those standing before me intently, noting what they were doing, so I could ape them and not make a fool of myself when it was my turn. You take a tray, point to the dishes you want, move to the cutlery trolley to get your fork, your spoon and your knife, go to a table, then sit down and eat. It seemed simple but daunting to me, because I had never done this before.

The big, tall canteen women in yellow uniforms might simply be doing their job, but I imagined impatience and exasperation from those piercing blue eyes as I fumbled about, pointing hastily at a couple of dishes. I wasn't sure what they were or what was in them but I was afraid of holding up the queue.

My sister Ba taught Linh and me how to use knives and forks. She learned this at the French Lycee.

'You shouldn't place your elbows on the table. When you want to finish the last bit of soup in the bowl, don't hold the bowl up, then tip the soup into your mouth and slurp the way Asians often do. Leave the bowl on the table, tilt it lightly and gracefully, like so, and scoop the soup with a spoon elegantly — *elegantly*.' Ba repeated this important point. 'Don't let the spoon touch the bowl or make a loud scraping noise like some half-starved person who cannot bear the thought of leaving the last bit of the soup at the bottom of the bowl to waste. To indicate that you are still eating, rest the tips of the knife and the fork on the two sides of your plate, the fork on your left, the knife on your right. When you are finished, place them in parallel with each other on the plate, the fork on the left, the knife on the right, the fork tines pointing up, not down, the sharp blade of the knife faced inwards, not outwards.'

'And the spoon? What to do with the spoon?'

'You place it between the knife and the fork.'

'Its hollow part faces up or down?'

'Hmmm…I'm not sure.'

If even Ba, the expert in Western eating etiquette, was not sure about this, then no wonder I was utterly confused.

The lesson continued.

'Take sugar for your tea or coffee with the small spoon. Have your soup with the big spoon. The small knife is to butter the bread. The big knife is reserved for the main meal, to cut the meat and the vegetables into small chunks. Do not confuse the one with the other. And don't cut the meat and the vegetables into bite-sized bits all at once. Only cut one piece at a time, and finish that before cutting another piece.'

These rules were surely much more complicated than using chopsticks.

In due time I would find that 'finger lickin' good' was totally acceptable, as far as KFC fried chicken was concerned. What a relief!

The following day, I woke up to the first Australian morning of my life, to the brightest sun, the greenest grass, the purest air with a soul-soothing hint of eucalyptus, and that precious feeling that had eluded me for a long time—the feeling of being safe.

However after my trip to the canteen for breakfast, I came back to my room feeling deflated. I knew the reason for my change of mood.

It had something to do with a fierce-looking canteen worker with fiery red hair and bright red lips who heaped a ladle of cereals into my bowl the way one chucks something into the dustbin, a despising look on her face.

I was pretty sure I had not done anything untoward. I tended to be self-conscious at the best of times. Now, being a refugee, I had nothing to feel confident about. I wondered if I was being overly sensitive, as insecure people tended to be, but clearly that lady didn't like me, and as she treated other Vietnamese the same way, I had a fair inkling she simply didn't like any of us. I struggled with the idea that a stranger could dislike me for no apparent reason at all. I wondered if she knew what we had been through.

In normal circumstances, perhaps I could simply dismiss this incident. There were unfriendly people in this world and we did run into them sometimes. However the circumstances that brought me to Australia were not normal, and this was only my second day in this country. Clearly I was in a fragile state and the slightest thing could tip me off balance.

For the rest of the day, I stayed inside the flat and only emerged to face the world at meal times. Even the endearing Australian sun outside could not help my mood. My head was crowded with depressing thoughts. The morning joy had evaporated. Having fallen in love with Australia at first sight, I preferred to stay in that blissful state for a bit longer. I preferred not to face reality too soon, especially when that reality consisted of overwhelming difficulties that could just drown me in self-pity.

My English was not even rudimentary; it was non-existent. How was I going to study? How was I going to work? What hope did I have when even a canteen worker looked down on me? What would the future hold for me?

None of these questions restored my spirit. I felt lost. I felt scared.

The efficient Australian social machine would soon incorporate the newcomers into its system. As unlikely as it might sound, apparently it was the Australian bureaucracy that saved my mood.

There were forms to fill and things to do. Register for social benefit, enroll in English classes, open a bank account, obtain health insurance, attend a health check... Most of these procedures and services were foreign to me.

The paper work kept me busy. I had no time to sit down feeling sorry for myself.

A stroll along well-paved streets near the hostel led me to an exciting discovery: a mobile library. It was located just outside the local High Point Shopping Centre.

I had been deprived of good books for too long. Following their victory, the Communists ordered the destruction of all South Vietnam's intellectual and cultural products in various cultural cleansing campaigns and replaced them with propaganda. Even text books and dictionaries did not escape the burning because they did not contain politically correct messages. A new Vietnamese-English dictionary would include examples such as 'to lash out at neo-colonialism', or 'socialism has now won the hearts and minds of thousands of millions in the world', to illustrate the use of the expression 'to lash out' and the verb 'to win' in a sentence. Primary school kids learned to solve math problems such as 'the anti-aircraft unit A shot down two American planes, the anti-aircraft unit B shot down three American planes, how many planes has the American enemy lost?' Literature and history lessons only taught about the communist revolution in Vietnam and abroad. In French lessons, we did not learn about French culture, but Party propaganda written in French.

My family's library was destroyed in a fire by the Communist soldiers who occupied our house.

Book lovers would understand my emotions when I stepped into the mobile library—a small caravan that had lots of books in it—for the first time. Like a starving person on a long and desperate trek in search for food, who suddenly chances on a hidden storage filled with hunks of leg hams and loaves of bread, it took me a moment to take in the marvellous sight in front of my eyes: books of all sizes and colours on steel shelves affixed to the caravan walls or displayed in small rotating stands. I felt happy and elated, as though I had just been reunited with a long-lost friend. I could not wait to re-enter the wonderful world of imagination and adventure.

With a jolt in my heart, I recognised all the familiar comic series such as The Smurfs, Lucky Luck, Tintin, and my favourite Asterix and Obelix. I had read them in French and Vietnamese. I could now learn to read them in English with the help of a dictionary. I chuckled at the familiar jokes. I recalled how my friends and I would pore over them at school recess.

The young female librarian with a sweet face and long golden hair smiled at me as I carried my pile of comics to the loan counter. Her warm and friendly manner gave me the impression that she liked my choice of books. Perhaps she was a fan of these series herself. I wondered if she knew how much she and her humble mobile library had brightened up my day.

The hostel's grocery store also operated as a bank agency. My brother, my sisters and I went there to cash our first special allowance cheque. We immediately splurged on M&M chocolates and Coke. Tasting them again reminded me of a happy time when my country was free.

Who could resist those attractively packaged Australian snacks on the store shelves such as Smiths potato chips and Nobby's nuts? I just *had* to try them. Wasn't it interesting — Australian roasted peanuts tasted exactly like those peddled by street sellers in my hometown!

That weekend we joined a horde of hostel residents flocking to the trash-and-treasure market. Like a mountain tribe descending on the big city for the first time, this excited and oddly dressed crowd simply stood out from the surroundings. The shy ones looked scared even when crossing the street, the bolder ones commented loudly for all to hear on the strange Australian things that came to their notice.

The trash–and–treasure market was a huge, bitumen-surfaced area the size of a sports oval. It was covered with a myriad of wonderful things that immediately appealed to this peculiar group of shoppers. The women and the girls went straight to mounts and racks of second-hand clothes. The men and the boys hovered near stereo sets, asking for their prices in broken English.

The cars that parked here had been turned into variety stores. Their doors and boot lids were left wide open. All sorts of bric-a-brac, old books, old shoes, cheap jewellery and odd-shaped ornaments competed for space on car seats and in car boots. A medley of things whose functions and usefulness might not be immediately obvious to ordinary folks were neatly arranged on foldable tables or dumped willy-nilly on huge tarpaulin spreads on the ground. The refugees picked this and that up, went from one store to another, seemingly unable to contain their excitement, while the traders stood leaning on their cars or sat in canvas chairs, quietly observed their potential customers with benign eyes, letting them scour through their wares nonchalantly, as though getting a sale or not was of no consequence to them.

I remembered Saigon's 'running markets' – so named because the sellers there were constantly on the run from the security police. Depending on the stocks they were carrying, only some shops were allowed to trade. Others were banned. People who resorted to selling their own possessions to buy food for their family in this desperate time risked being fined or having their goods confiscated for committing an illegal act of trading without permission. To buy and sell to make money and earn a profit, normal human activities since biblical times, were now branded 'capitalist' and 'reactionary'. Most of the 'reactionary capitalists' were destitute women whose husbands were languishing in 're-education camps'—the politically correct term for Communist jails. They needed to clinch a sale because that would mean their kids would not go hungry that night. Compared with that depressed and heartbroken atmosphere, this market resembled a picnic.

Soft music came from a car's radio. A stout woman pointed to a handwritten sign '3 for $1' on a piece of cardboard placed on top of her clothes pile. I sat down and made my choice. I could not believe that with just $1 dollar, I could afford a whole outfit.

In my home town the Communist ration was two metres of coarse fabric for every two persons, once per year. As two metres of fabric could only make one pair of pants, two people had to share it. Logic decreed that half the population would have to go half-naked from the waist down while waiting for their turn to wear these *Communist pants.* The true spirit of communism had thus been manifested; everything was shared among the people, pants included. Long live Chairman Ho Chi Minh!

I received forty dollars in special allowance every fortnight. Thirty dollars were automatically deducted to pay for meals and accommodation at the hostel, the rest was deposited in my bank account.

With my first ten dollars in the bank, I started my savings plan. I never spent all of my allowance. I made sure to save at least two dollars each fortnight. Two dollars this fortnight plus two dollars next fortnight equalled four dollars; you could not go wrong with the maths. The balance in my bank account kept increasing. This was my first step towards building my financial nest. My father always drummed into the children, both boys and girls, the importance of being financially independent in life. My mother, who was always extremely careful with money, should be very proud of me.

Up until this point in my life, money was not something I had ever needed to be concerned about. Back in Dalat, I manned Mother's shop and handled the daily takings. I carried large amounts of cash in my trips to Saigon to buy merchandise for the shop, but I never had any pocket money. If I needed anything, I would just ask Mother.

Now I counted every cent in my pocket because I worried about my future.

I had some talent in Vietnamese literature and the French language, the two subjects that helped me achieve top rankings at school. They were totally useless in this English-speaking country. I sat down and made a list of what other skills I had to fall back on and came to a crushing realisation—there was none.

What could I do and how would I be able to support myself, let alone realising my plan to go to university? Finishing university had always been my goal. Now I was not so sure.

I made the mistake of confiding my fear about the future to a Vietnamese man in my English class. He seemed to be a decent chap.

'Women are only good for one thing.'

He mentioned the French expression *bonne a marier*. 'You can always get married,' he smirked.

I checked his face to make sure this was simply a lousy joke. No, he was not smiling. I walked away from him, furious.

Learning English was the first mountain I had to climb. There were day classes and night classes. I went to both. The teachers were kind, patient and supportive. My classmates, a mixed group of refugees from Vietnam and migrants from various parts of Europe, all different ages and backgrounds, gave me an interesting first insight into Australia's culturally diverse society.

I sat next to Peter, a Pole, in a day class. He seemed likeable enough until one day he confided in me, 'Asians like you are all right, but I don't like black people.' He did not faze when I frowned, rolled my eyes and shook my head in disapproval. 'The blacks, they are really not nice,' he insisted.

His female compatriot, Helena, did not seem to share this discriminatory view. Her flat was opposite mine. She had frequent male visitors.

One time a seemingly distinguished African man in a sharp, three-piece suit knocked on the door of my flat and asked for Helena. I pointed to the door behind him.

I did not think much about this incident until a few weeks later. My English class went on an excursion to a nice park. The teacher took pictures, brought them to class and gave each student a couple of photos to keep. Helena was absent on that day. I volunteered to bring them to her after class.

Helena opened the door and invited me in. The interior of her flat was exactly like mine. A short and narrow corridor led to tiny rooms on its right and on its left, each room had a single bed and a table-and-chair set.

I stood at the doorstep of her room.

An Australian male, much younger than Helena, perhaps in his twenties, was sitting at one end of her bed. I sensed his uneasiness when he saw me. I was not quite sure what was the nature of their relationship and so hesitated as to how I should greet him, and whether I should enter her room at all.

On the wall opposite her bed hung a huge poster of a naked woman in a shocking pose.

That, and something in the way Helena glanced at me, gave me a pretty clear idea as to why she had so many male visitors. I quickly handed her the photos and left.

There were other subterranean activities at the hostel which, at the time, totally escaped me.

The parking space in front of the grocery store was the hostel's unofficial meeting place. After dark, Australian men from outside would come in their cars and park here. They would befriend some male residents at the hostel, both young and old, who happened to hang around the car park at that time. One time I went to the store to get some snacks. I overheard a Vietnamese man telling his friends that an Australian man seemed to 'like' his younger brother 'very much' and kept showering him with gifts. His younger brother felt 'pity' for the Australian, who was quite insistent, but he just could not accept them. I listened in but failed to detect any sinister undertone, thinking to myself how nice these locals were towards refugees.

Life at the hostel was quite pleasant once I got used to its daily routine. Having been through so many upheavals, I welcomed it. Daily routine gave structure to my life and provided me with a much needed sense of stability.

Ten days after our arrival at the hostel, Linh enrolled in a nearby school, Maribyrnong High. The rest of us attended English classes at the hostel. I delighted in simple weekend pleasures such as curling up in bed with a book, taking a stroll in quiet streets near the hostel with my brother and sisters, window shopping at High Point Shopping Centre on Saturday to marvel at all the beautiful and expensive things we envied but could not afford, and going to the trash-and-treasure market on Sunday to look for another '3 for $1' bargain.

The hostel staff took care of room cleaning and changing the bed sheets; hostel residents only needed to wash their own clothes. Each block of flats had a communal laundry equipped with washing machines, clothes dryers, and a couple of rotary clothes hoists outside the laundry. I did not know the rotary clothes hoist was a unique Australian icon; I simply thought it was such a good idea. It spun in the wind, the clothes drying more quickly this way.

The hostel, the streets surrounding it, and the short distance from the hostel to High Point Shopping Centre and the trash-and-treasure market—this summed up my knowledge about Australia at this point in time. Coming from the dire poverty of a Communist country, this tiny fragment of Australia's larger society already impressed me. The endless varieties of merchandise in the shops; a thousand types of food and drinks packed on supermarket shelves; a mountain of goods sold at unbelievable prices at the trash-and-treasure market. If someone had told me this area was among Melbourne's poorer suburbs and this material abundance was merely basic comfort for ordinary, even lower class Australians, I might not have believed them. The magnitude of Australia's richness was beyond my imagination.

How on earth had I never heard of this amazing country before? I recalled asking Ba where is Australia when we were in the refugee camp. I could only shake my head in disbelief at my former ignorance. I could laugh at it now.

I grew to love Australian food which, unsurprisingly, was very different to Vietnamese cuisine. Roast lamb was a novelty to me because Vietnamese don't eat lamb. Tasting rice pudding required some mental adjustment because in Vietnamese cooking, rice was a main staple food to be consumed with savoury dishes. Meat dishes, like lamb roast, using something unmistakably sweet like plum jam as a condiment amused me no end. To me it was such a departure from the norm, as odd as having lollies for main course. I'd had a fixed idea as to how certain ingredients should be prepared or eaten. The meals at the canteen were an enjoyable way for me to appreciate that beyond the narrow confines of what I had known and had been accustomed to all my life, there existed many other exciting possibilities.

Not all Vietnamese were fond of Australian cuisine like me. Some Vietnamese missed the spicy Asian taste so badly that they would go to the trouble to get packets of instant noodles from the supermarket, purchase a second-hand electric cooking device from the trash-and-treasure market, then wait for an opportune time to boil water and make themselves a bowl of instant noodles in their flat. It must be just the way they liked it: with a squeeze of lemon, a sprinkle of hot pepper, a dash of Maggi soy sauce, and slices of tongue-biting hot chilli. They certainly kidded themselves if they thought that the cleaners would not notice a spicy smell the moment they entered their flat, or fail to find the incriminating cooking device cleverly hidden in such an obvious place—the clothes cupboard. The cooking utensil would be temporarily confiscated and returned to the owner when his stay at the hostel came to an end. The hostel management specifically banned people from cooking in their flats.

For many new migrants, and certainly for me, coming to Australia and living in the hostel was the first time I had ever come into contact with people of different cultures from far away continents and got to know them in a more than superficial way. English class was fun because besides learning the language, I got the chance to listen to other students' life stories. English was spoken with a variety of accents, not always grammatically correct, but we all laughed at the same jokes and shared the same dream. We all wanted to master the language, learn more about this country that had generously taken us in, settle in as quickly as possible, and make something of ourselves in this land.

The hostel normally allowed families to stay for six months. Singles were given three months. My family's six-month limit was approaching.

The idea that we would leave this protective environment and be out in the real Australian world was both scary and liberating.

A Catholic nun from St John's church came to our assistance.

Sister Power was a frequent and reassuring presence at the hostel. She walked with a swift gait and a slight stoop. Her tiny frame always seemed to be in motion. Well past her sixties, yet she never showed any sign she might need to slow down. Many hostel residents sought her help. She made time to talk and listen attentively to each and every one of them. She carried in her shoulder bag a small inventory consisting of items a newly arrived person would need and she would be happy to give them out: free aerogrammes, face washers, toothbrushes and toothpaste.

My sisters and I met her when we were on our way to the hostel's post office. She talked to us and was delighted that my older sister Ba could speak decent English with her. I took an immediate liking to her. She reminded me of my French teacher, who was also a Catholic nun. We mentioned to her that our stay at the hotel was coming to an end and that we were looking for a place to move out.

Later on that day Sister Power came to our flat, perhaps as part of her fact finding mission to see if we genuinely deserved assistance. We opened the clothes cupboards and showed her all we had: some nondescript clothing items that we brought with us from the refugee camp and a few recent acquisitions from the trash-and-treasure market.

Soon after her visit, Sister Power told us she had found a place for us.

If your entire possessions could be tossed nicely into a few green rubbish bags, moving houses is quite simple. Clutching these in our hands, we boarded a bus and got off, as instructed, at a bus stop in a quiet street in Ascot Vale.

Following a handwritten map, we walked to a lovely house painted in white in Kent Street. This would be our first home in Australia.

Sister Power and the people from St John's church must have been organizing our move for some time. When we arrived, a small team of volunteers were still busy arranging and re-arranging things, giving the house a finishing touch. They waved and smiled at us and we shyly waved and smiled back.

Karen, a sweet-looking young lady with striking blue eyes and wavy golden hair, introduced herself to us and gave us a tour of the house. The rooms were huge, the ceiling was high, sunlight flooded in through the tall double-hung windows.

I had not been in a great mood having to move out of the hostel. Compared with the refugee camp, it was five-star accommodation to me. I had settled in nicely and did not want any change to my daily routine. Only when I stepped into our new home did I realise how tiny our former flat was. Everything is relative. I loved the spacious feel of the new house. Already I felt an uplifting in my spirits.

The house was furnished with good second-hand furniture and second-hand household articles. Anything that we would need, someone had already thought of it. Clearly many people had generously spent a lot of their time and effort going around asking for donations, organising transport, and setting things up nicely in the house for us.

All the beds had been perfectly made; I could never make my bed this well. Karen smiled at my genuine admiration. She said she worked as a nurse at St Vincent's Hospital and making beds was part of her training. She undid one end of the bed and showed me how to achieve the crisp 'hospital corners'.

There were fluffy, brand new bath towels in the bathroom and pots, pans and cutlery in the kitchen cupboard.

Back in Vietnam the Communists chose the houses they liked. The house owners and their families were thrown out in the street. This happened to my family. Here in Australia, strangers came to our aid and gave us this beautifully furnished house - just like that.

All we needed to do was to live in it.

I was overwhelmed with gratitude and yet a shy 'thank you' was all I could mutter. I felt disappointed at not being able to express my appreciation more adequately. My non-existent English and my inherent shyness rendered me tongue-tied and aggravated my clumsiness.

Our landlord was a middle-aged Italian man with a stocky build and a quiet demeanour. He often came to the house in his white overalls to carry out maintenance work. The number of tenants allowed under the lease contract was a mystery to me, but it was not unusual for the landlord to find a crowd just shy of a dozen at any one time in this three-bedroom house every time he turned up. A few friends joined us when their stay at the hostel ended. The landlord generously turned a blind eye to this, allowing us to save on rental and living expenses because they were now shared among more people.

The house had only one bathroom and one toilet—the toilet was inside the bathroom—for all of us. The rickety outdoor toilet in the back garden often saved someone from some very tricky moments.

Our Australian neighbours often waved and said hello to us. An elderly lady who lived a few doors from us saw me in the street. She invited me to her house for afternoon tea. I got to see the interior of an Australian house for the first time. What might be considered as basic comfort and regular Australian house features impressed me as superbly elegant: the wallpapered walls, the thick carpeted floor, and the imposing lounge suite placed opposite a marble fireplace. I had never seen wallpapered walls, wall-to-wall carpeted floors and a marble fireplace before. I could not take my eyes off the artful leadlight windows. Even people considered well off in my town did not have these luxuries. The lady was in her seventies, her hair a well-coiffed perm; she looked graceful in a beige dress and a matching beige cardigan.

'Would you like a cup of tea? Or coffee, dear?' she asked.

'Yes, may I have tea, please. Thanks,' I said.

This simple exchange was in fact a cultural shift for me.

In Vietnamese culture, it is considered impolite for a visitor to accept the offer of food or drink by the host when being asked the first time. By refusing it the first time, the visitor shows the host that he respects him and is reluctant to impose on him, at the same time displaying his self-respect and self-control.

In a society that values Confucius-inspired noble intentions, a pre-occupation with worldly desires such as food and drink can be interpreted as a character failure.

Yes, there is such a thing as the cultural divide.

Australians, and Westerners in general, look directly at the person they are talking to in order to show they are open, honest and respectful. Vietnamese in traditional societies, on the other hand, avert direct eye contact to show respect. In feudal times, commoners bowed their heads and looked at their feet when talking to the mandarins of the royal court. Children lowered their gazes in the presence of parents, students in the presence of teachers. To look straight at those of higher status than you could give the impression that you saw yourself as their equal, which might be construed as insolent or presumptuous.

Australians and Vietnamese seem to be at opposite ends in gender protocol. In Vietnam, people of opposite sex are not supposed to have skin to skin contact with each other, such as holding hands, kissing or embracing in public. Anything of a sexual or intimate nature should be confined in the bedroom. However, people of the same gender can hold hands or wrap their arms around each other's shoulders in public, as these are considered gestures of friendship. Foreigners who visit Vietnam but are not aware of this might think that it is a country of rampant homosexuality.

Curiously, while homosexuality is still an issue for debate in several Western countries, it has not gained much attention in Vietnamese mainstream consciousness. Homosexual people in Vietnam do not seem to suffer severe social stigma as they do in some other countries. The poet Xuan Dieu is famous for his love poems, most of which were dedicated to the various men in his life. The writer Ho Truong An is another well-known Vietnamese who does not hide his homosexuality. The two men are widely admired for their talent; their sexual preference did not seem to affect their social standing. I remember studying Xuan Dieu's writing at high school – *young women are beautiful like flowers, young men are beautiful like leaves.* No one raised an eyebrow at that.

One of the more memorable characters that I met in Kota Bharu camp was a homosexual young man. He possessed a sweet singing voice and often delighted the crowd with emotion-laden songs often sung by female singers. That endeared him to many camp dwellers and turned him into a bit of a mini-celebrity. No one questioned his sexuality. People only asked him whether he would prefer to be addressed as 'brother' or 'sister'. And he would say, 'It's fine by me either way.'

Vietnamese do not have the equivalent of the gender neutral and age neutral pronoun 'you' to refer to the person, or persons that one is talking to. Titles of address such as 'brother', 'sister' are not only used among family members and relatives, but also to address unrelated people, depending on their age, as a mark of respect. In the case of this young man, his gender preference needed to be established so the right term of address could be used.

In countries where homosexual people are stigmatised, even brutalised, the correct title of address would be the least of their concerns. Compared with these, Vietnamese society seems to be much more accepting and open-minded. Yet it stays ultra-conservative in eschewing public displays of affection, even between heterosexual couples.

In English classes the teachers often encouraged the students to discuss aspects of Australian culture they found strange or different from their own.

'I went to an Australian friend's house the other day. She asked me whether I would like to have any tea or coffee. I said no and ended up not having any,' one Vietnamese lady in my class complained.

The male teacher was clearly amused.

'But you said no, didn't you?'

'Yes, but I was only being polite. Of course I would like some tea, but once I said no, she didn't offer it to me again.'

The students from European countries such as Hungary or Poland could not contain their chuckles, while the Vietnamese and the Chinese-Vietnamese in the class nodded their heads in shared understanding.

'Well, for Australians, when you say no, we would take it that you really mean no. Otherwise you would have said yes, wouldn't you?' the teacher asked.

This explanation of the obvious made the Europeans chuckle again, while the Asians looked puzzled, as though they were still not convinced by this kind of stark logic.

Thanks to this class discussion, I did not commit any *faux-pas* when I visited my neighbour. I said yes right away when she offered me a drink and looked directly at her when we talked.

The lady brought out tea and biscuits in a nice china set on a silver tray. The memory of eating cooked rice out of a sad looking plastic bowl with a bent aluminium spoon in the refugee camp was still fresh in my mind. There was something unreal about me sitting in a comfortable lounge room in a nice house in a Melbourne suburb, sipping tea with a graceful Australian lady on a tranquil afternoon. I couldn't help feeling like an intruder, someone who was teleported to a distant place by an accidental press of a button, acutely conscious of that fact and hoping no one would mind my incongruous presence.

PART IV
A SORROWFUL VICTORY

The many kind and compassionate Australians who went out of their way to help me and my family when we first came to the country gave me a wonderful first impression about Australia. For a newcomer to a strange land, the feeling of being welcome and accepted is important. I thrived on it and I am ever grateful for it.

Only decades later, when I had the chance to talk to more people and read more books, that I realised that the Vietnamese presence in Australia in the aftermath of the Vietnam War was as controversial as the war itself.

During the Vietnam War years, according to Gerard Henderson, 'it was fashionable to support the Communist victories in Indochina. This was the position of most leading figures of the Australian left including Prime Minister Gough Whitlam, Deputy Prime Minister Jim Cairns, the Deputy Leader of the Australian Labor Party Tom Uren, and the overwhelming majority of academics, journalists and other opinion leaders involved in the public debate on Australia's Vietnam commitment'.[24]

For Clyde Cameron, a Communist victory in Vietnam meant 'the right side had won'.[25]

The refugees, no matter how tragic their situation, were perceived unfavourably for being on the 'wrong side'.

Extreme terms had been used to describe them - capitalists and enemies of Communist liberation, or worse, extreme right-wing racketeers, drug-peddlers, procurers, prostitutes, and possible carriers of venereal disease.[26]

No wonder Australian Prime Minister Gough Whitlam did not warm to the idea of giving Vietnamese refugees asylum in Australia. According to Clyde Cameron, Whitlam said to Don Willesee, in his presence, in 1975: 'I'm not having hundreds of f..king Vietnamese Balts coming into this country with their religious and political hatreds against us'.[27] Whitlam did not dispute Cameron's account.[28]

A Special Statement of the 1979 Tokyo Summit described the plight of Indochinese refugees as a 'humanitarian problem of historic proportion'. At the Association of Southeast-Asian Nations (ASEAN) annual meeting in February 1979, Filipino Foreign Minister Carlos Romulo compared Hanoi's policy towards Vietnamese refugees with Hitler's systematic murder of the Jews and described it as 'another form of inhumanity, equal in scope and similarly heinous' as the Holocaust. Singaporean Foreign Minister Sinnathamby Rajaratnam was scathing about the Vietnamese Communists' policy towards the Boat People. 'A poor man's alternative to the gas chambers is the open sea,' he said.[29]

Despite these powerful statements, international opinion remained divided.

While Joan Baez and 83 other former anti-war activists published an open letter criticizing Hanoi's serious violations of human rights following its takeover of South Vietnam, Jane Fonda remained a steadfast supporter of the Communists. Not only she refused to sign public petitions in support of the Boat People,[30] she wrote to Baez denouncing the latter for criticizing the Hanoi regime: *'Such rhetoric only aligns you with the narrow and negative elements in our country who continue to believe that communism is worse than death.'*[31]

The famous philosopher Jean-Paul Sartre, a staunch Marxist, was a surprise champion for Boat People. He appealed to the French government to help Vietnamese refugees: *'Some of them have not always been on our side, but for the moment we are not interested in their politics, but in saving their lives. It's a moral issue, a question of morality between human beings.'* [32]

Benedict O'Donohoe was of the view that Sartre's profound moral instincts and his belief in the inalienability of human freedom were behind this change of heart.[33]

However Sartre and Baez were among a minority. Most US anti-war activists were 'incredibly silent' and 'strangely quiescent' when it came to the Boat People tragedy and Hanoi's human rights record.[34] This prompted the great Russian writer Alexander Solzhenitsyn to voice his indignation:

'But members of the US anti-war movement wound up being involved in the betrayal of Far Eastern nations, in a genocide and in the suffering today imposed on 30 million there. Do those convinced pacifists hear the moans coming from there? Do they understand their responsibility today? Or they prefer not to hear?'[35]

Liu Shaoqi, chief theoretician of the Chinese Communist Party, said that morality was not relevant when dealing with capitalist counter-revolutionaries. According to him, moralists did not believe in the class struggle and so were consequently anti-Marxist.[36]

Those judged as enemy of the proletarian revolution should expect no mercy.

North Vietnamese poet Nguyen Chi Thien knew this very well, from his broken life. He had the temerity to tell the truth about life under communism, which diverged greatly from propaganda:

> *In this land, a joyless land*
> *People wipe sweat off their faces during the day*
> *Then wipe the tears from their eyes at night*
> *Boot camps and prisons*

These are where people end up in droves
So, so few ever return
Perhaps five, perhaps three
Hungry children turn pale
Toil the land is now women's tasks
The village's men have all gone
Death notices are scattered in the air
Like leaflets dropped from a plane
Over the thatched huts roofs
There is nothing
Nothing, but sadness in this land
Except for the uplifting propaganda
Blaring out from the P.A. system!

Nguyen Chi Thien was locked up for twenty-seven years in the hellish Vietnamese gulags:

I urge the world
Please come and see with your own eyes
The concentration camps hidden in deep forests and rugged terrains
Here, like animals
Herds of prisoners line up to wash next to each other
Without a shred of rag on them to cover up their emaciated bodies
They share their dank and filthy cells
With bed bugs and mosquitoes
They fight with each other
Over a measly bit of potato or cassava
Their fates are linked with shackles, summary arrests,
With being hacked and stabbed multiple times
With violent bashing and gratuitous assaults

> *If any of them dies*
> *Who cares*
> *The dead body would be dragged away, somewhere,*
> *For the rats to feast on*
> *These prisoners are modern-day chimpanzees*
> *That bear no resemblance to human relatives of pre-historic time*
> *They are not nimble but painfully slow*
> *They are only skin and bones because of the constant hunger*
> *And yet, miraculously, they are super-productive*
> *The government reaps the fruit of their hard labour*
> *All year round.*
> *I urge the world*
> *Please come and visit North Vietnam*
> *To see how quickly man regresses back to chimp!*

Once the war had been won, Hanoi swiftly threw away the heartfelt nationalistic rhetoric. In 1976, one year after 'reunification', in his speech at the 25th Party's Central Committee conference, Le Duan affirmed the true nature of his regime: '*Our regime is a dictatorship of the proletariat. The policy of our dictatorship, first and foremost, is the policy of the proletariat. This is the most scientific policy, it strictly follows the law of nature, everyone must swear allegiance to it. This policy is absolutely uncompromising, it does not share power with anyone and does not cooperate with anyone... This is the policy of the working class, no one is allowed to resist it. Whoever resists it will be arrested.*'[37]

What started as a utopian vision of the world had come down to this.

Decades on, more information had come out from behind the bamboo curtain that shed new light on the twenty-year long conflict.

During the Vietnam War, over 320,000 Chinese soldiers were sent to North Vietnam to serve on the home front, so the North could send more of its own troops to the South. When China withdrew its troops from Vietnam in August 1973, 1,100 Chinese soldiers had been killed and 4,200 had been wounded. China's supply of material resources in Vietnam was enormous. Besides weapons and military equipment, China provided North Vietnamese troops with hundreds of food and non-food items, including hundreds of tons of rice, meat, fish, sugar, uniforms, shoes, cigarettes, right down to toothbrushes, toothpaste and sewing needles.[38]

In September 1975, after the Communist victory, Duan took a trip to Beijing to thank Mao: 'Our country has never experienced a greater joy than this. Without China, our great and vast home front, without Chairman Mao's directives and policies, without our Chinese comrades' aid, we could not have won the War'.[39]

It was naïve to think that China helped Vietnam purely out of a shared idealistic vision of the world. China's relationship with Vietnam waxed and waned depending on its ideological and geopolitical interests.[40]

It threw its weight behind North Vietnam when it wanted to eliminate America's presence in South Vietnam, weaken America's influence in Southeast Asia and spread the communist doctrine in Indochina.[41] Following the Communist victory over South Vietnam, China's geopolitical interests changed. It disapproved of Vietnam's close ties with Russia and its hegemonic ambition in the region. It cut off aid to Vietnam and switched support to the anti-Vietnamese Khmer Rouge. In 1979 it sent troops over the border 'to teach Vietnam a lesson' for its foray in Cambodia.

The Soviet Union also provided great support to North Vietnam during the Vietnam War. Voice of Russia, Vietnamese language program, reported that over 10,000 Vietnamese officers received training in various Soviet Union military universities, many of whom would take a leadership role in Vietnam's air force and air-defence force. During the last 10 years of the War, from 1965 to 1974, around 6,500 Soviet Union generals and officers, and 5,000 Soviet Union soldiers and corporals served in Vietnam. The Soviet Union suffered 13 fatalities in the Vietnam War, including 4 military experts who died in the battlefield and 6 sailors who died on their way to deliver aid to Vietnam. Throughout the War - dubbed the anti-American war of resistance by the communist camp - North Vietnam received on average 40 shiploads of aid each month from the Soviet Union. Vietnam downed 1,300 American aircrafts thanks to Soviet missiles, fought air battles with MiG aircrafts, used Kalashnikov rifles AK-47 in ground battles. It was a Soviet tank, a T-55, that crashed through the gate of South Vietnam's President Palace on the historic day of the communist victory on 30 April 1975.[42]

When Beijing reneged on its promise to provide aid to Vietnam for post-war reconstruction, Moscow generously stepped in with a reported $3 billion in aid and grants for Vietnam's Five-Year Plan.[43] Vietnam relied on Soviet aid and weapons to topple the China-backed Khmer Rouge. When China carried an all-out attack on Vietnam in 1979, the Soviet Union helped Vietnam counter their common enemy. Besides playing the role of the big brother to the Vietnamese communists, Hanoi's allegiance helped the Soviet Union contain China and extend its influence in Southeast Asia.

Over three million Vietnamese from both the North and the South died in the Vietnam War. For whom, and for what?

According to the well-known author Vu Thu Hien, Le Duan had proclaimed: 'We fight the Americans for the Soviet Union, for China, for the socialist countries and the whole of mankind'.[44]

This proclamation furthers the line of reasoning that the Vietnamese communists were willing useful idiots who served China's and the Soviet Union's strategy in Southeast Asia.

When China sent 600,000 troops to invade Vietnam in 1979,[45] the international solidarity of the proletariat spirit must be furthest in its mind.

The Vietnam War was, and remains, a controversial issue. The Communist victory in 1975 meant different things to different people.

While communist supporters in the West were jubilant, Nguyen Chi Thien, in his dark cell, wept:

> *Oh South Vietnam, ever since the day of your loss*
> *I have experienced a thousand, ten thousand agonies!*

On 30 April 1975, the South Vietnamese poet Nguyen Mau Lam was literally roused out of his sleep to the realisation that his country had just been 'liberated'. He recalled that historic day:

> *The thirtieth of April nineteen seventy five*
> *At three o'clock in the morning*
> *It is still pitch dark*
> *The heavy fog blurs my vision*
> *Already a lout from the local security police goes around the neighbourhood,*
> *He pounces on the door of each and every house and screams at the top of his lungs:*
> *'Wake up! Wake up quickly! Meeting!'*
> *Reluctantly, I wake up.*
> *'Okay, if you force me to, I'll go.'*
> *Already there's a crowd in front of the security police office*
> *People hunch over and wrap their arms around their bodies*
> *It's freezing cold*
> *They stand still*

Traces of a rudely interrupted sleep remain on their faces

Like rows of graves in a cemetery

They stay quiet

Except for the lout from the security police

Who cannot keep his trap shut

He yells

He screams

His yelling and screaming resonate in the quiet early morning:

'Kids? This line!'

'Teens? This line!'

'Women, this line!'

'Men, this line!'

'Monks, priests, you hopeless bunch, this line!'

'And the lackeys who worked for the previous government, you come here! Come here!'

We are graves that can move

Cadavers that can shudder in the cold

We start marching and reach the city square at five o'clock in the morning

Crowds and crowds of people are pouring to this place

They stand in silent rows

Little kids stand leaning on each other's shoulders, still half-asleep

Some grown-ups even have to sit on the earth floor

At nine o'clock in the morning

The meeting starts

Everyone

Feet together, stand up straight

'Shun'

We welcome you, comrade Chief of the Party Delegate

And other comrades
Including comrade Provincial Committee Party Secretary
Comrade Chief of the People Committee
And the comrades who arrive late
All the comrades take their seats on the lofty high platform
The singing begins
It is compulsory for everyone to sing
'As though Uncle Ho were right here with us
On this joyful day of glorious victory…'
My mouth is unmoved.
The lout from the security police lunges towards me like a violent wind
'Sing! Sing! Mother f…ker you! Why don't you sing?'
Alright then, I'll sing
I mumble the song as though I am trying to chew some badly cooked rice
The lout from the security police screams at me, again:
'Sing loudly!'
I bleat, I croak, like a cane toad
It is compulsory for everyone to sing
I try hard to contain my tears
My heart is in searing pain
A boiling anger rises within me
I let out a quiet insult:
'F… you!'

***

Had the Whitlam government stayed in power in 1975, perhaps my life would have turned out very differently. Whitlam was dismissed from office towards the end of that year in controversial circumstances. This event was unrelated to the Vietnamese tragedy, however it would play a decisive role in the fate of tens of thousands of Vietnamese. The reason being, Malcolm Fraser, the man who succeeded Whitlam, had always been a staunch advocate for humane treatment of asylum seekers. While Whitlam considered putting Vietnamese asylum seekers who reached Australia by sea into custody, Fraser allowed them to land, gave them temporary residence permits a day after their arrival and permanent residence soon afterwards.[46] Under Malcolm Fraser's prime ministership, tens of thousands of South Vietnamese refugees were given the chance to start a new life in Australia.

Buddhists believe that all phenomena are interconnected. In the words of the astrophysicist Trinh Xuan Thuan, *the world is a vast flow of events that are linked together and participate in one another.*[47] The causal connection between the dismissal of an Australian Prime Minister and the fate of Vietnamese a continent away seemed to illustrate this point.

For refugees who were Catholic, Gough Whitlam's dismissal might be seen as divine intervention, and Malcolm Fraser, the prominent politician known for his toughness, might be an angel in disguise.

***

Looking back at the controversies, I wonder if parliamentarians and sections in the media that had adopted an anti-Vietnamese refugee stand had misread the Australian public. I have trouble reconciling their hostile views with the kindness and the generosity I received from Australians I met in those early years – especially from the people of St John's Catholic church, my English teachers, my neighbours, my landlord. They represented the Australia that I came to know and feel forever grateful for. I felt safe and protected in this cocoon of compassion. I refuse to think this was only a beautiful illusion. Even if it was, in hindsight, it was good for me. In my blissful ignorance, I could just focus on getting used to this new land. That was a hard enough task.

PART V
ONE STEP AT A TIME

If there was something less scary than starting a new life in a new country from scratch, it was not having to do it alone. If there was something less embarrassing than committing a blunder, it was having someone to laugh about it with you, not at you. Luckily, I had a little crowd consisting of my family and our friends at Kent Street who stumbled through life in those early days in Australia with me.

On our first trip to High Point Shopping Centre, we saw a policeman pointing his finger threateningly at us from afar. We all got scared and did not know what to do. Coming from an authoritarian country, our immediate thought was we had done something illegal. In Vietnam everything required permission from several layers of bureaucracy. Perhaps we needed permission to enter the shopping centre? We froze on the spot. The policeman did not move. The suspense was unbearable. Some minutes passed. This was ridiculous. We could not stand like this all day. We decided to approach the officer. 'He' turned out to be a realistic, life-sized cardboard replica of a policeman placed behind the shop window, perhaps an innovative way to deter thieves.

We took the bus to Footscray for the first time, got off and stood on the pavement for barely two minutes when we noticed the 'No Standing Any Time' sign. Its meaning was clear enough. Being new to the country, eager to prove that we were decent, law-abiding individuals, we duly obeyed the instruction and kept walking, only to find this sign many times again along the whole street. I felt tired having to keep on walking—this was one harsh rule, but what other possible explanation could there be for this simple sign? We noticed an Australian man who stood right next to the sign for some time; perhaps he was waiting for someone. He didn't seem at all concerned that he was doing something contrary to the law. We asked him whether he should *not stand here any time*. He said this sign was for cars.

It was a good thing that all of us, my family and our friends at Kent Street, were a driven and positive crowd. No one knew what the future would bring—we could not project our vision that far, and that was scary—but everyone was determined to make use of every opportunity that came their way, and not to waste time. We were taking one baby step at a time, but each step was a step forward. After one year in Australia, we all made good progress in our lives.

Thanks to their language ability, both my stepsister My and my older sister Ba found full-time employment as interpreters. Tens of thousands of Vietnamese refugees were allowed to settle in Australia from the late 1970s onwards; interpreters were in high demand. My little sister Linh thrived at Maribyrnong High. My stepbrother Tuan and my brother Chau worked in factories. Tin, his male friends and I were preparing for university.

There were several advanced English courses for those wanting to go to university. The teachers directed me to the ones they thought would be most helpful to me. Throughout my first year in Australia, English was my preoccupation. I would immerse myself in the nightmare of English grammar, verb tenses, tricky prepositions - a misuse of which would alter the whole meaning of a sentence. I tried to read as much as I could to build up my vocabulary. I was still not confident enough to converse in English, but having completed countless language exercises, I could at least string two words together on paper.

Having some spare time between English classes, I went looking for a part-time job.

A short tram ride brought me to Moonee Ponds Social Security office (it is now called Centrelink). The internet was non-existent then. Job cards were pinned on white boards. If you liked the job description on a card, you brought that card to a clerk who would provide you with more details and conduct a preliminary check to see if you were suitable.

I thought the position of 'shop assistant' for a clothes shop was mine to take. The female officer asked me if I had any relevant experience. I said back in Vietnam I often manned my mother's shop.

She shook her head. 'I think they need someone with Australian work experience.'

I brought another card to another officer, for a waitress job.

The man looked at the job description and frowned. 'I don't think this is suitable for you.'

'I can do it,' I said enthusiastically.

He shook his head. 'They are looking for someone to work at three am! You understand?'

The man's unhappy expression told me there was something not quite right about this 'job'.

Sensing I was still perplexed, he explained. 'Three am, that's three o'clock in the morning. Not three pm, which is in the afternoon. Try to look for a position that requires you to work at normal hours—during the day.'

'Oh, I didn't notice it. I thought it was three o'clock in the afternoon.' I was not used to this 'am' and 'pm' thing, the Australian way of telling the time.

There was another waitress job at a 'tavern' in North Melbourne. I double-checked to make sure there was nothing odd about the working hours before going there to apply in person. After two tram rides and a long walk in deserted back streets, I arrived at the 'tavern'. It was an unobtrusive brick building among other nondescript offices and shops. Its entrance was narrow, dark and uninviting. A lady with a high perm sat behind the counter.

Seeing me coming in, she looked up but didn't say anything.

Her unfriendly manner made me feel even more nervous. I forced a smile. 'I come to apply for the waitress job.'

She looked at me again from head to toe, then shook her head. I must look so out of place, so *foreign* to her with my heavy accent, my awkward manner, and the odd pieces of clothing from the trash-and-treasure market I had assembled on me.

This must have been the shortest job interview ever. I was clearly not what she was looking for.

Whatever 'job' this was, I didn't feel at all upset at the way I was swiftly, and non-verbally, rejected. The woman's offhandedness aside, there was something about the 'tavern' that made me feel uneasy and want to walk away from it as quickly as possible.

I didn't give up on my job quest. I went to a takeaway shop near Victoria Market in North Melbourne to apply for a sandwich hand position. I was successful this time.

I came from a country with chronic food scarcity. The Vietnamese government's policy was to keep the people in perpetual hunger so they could be turned into Pavlov's dogs, conditioned to think the only way they could have something to eat was to obey the Party unquestionably. The state-owned stores were normally closed. On rare occasions when there was something to distribute, the neighbourhood chief would go from street to street announcing this important news at the top of his voice, upon which people would drop everything to rush to the store so they would not miss out on the meagre ration. There was never more than one type of food to be given out at each distribution session, and the store never had enough for everyone. Unfailingly, after queuing for hours, there would be someone who would miss out on a few kilos of rice or a litre of low-grade fish sauce. The look of disappointment on their face was heartbreaking. The store attendants gave out these precious rations with an imperious air. The government used food to control the people. Those who served in food stores—a plum job usually reserved for the well connected – often let their petty power go to their heads.

Still new to Australia, I did not think I had fully grasped the extent of Australia's richness and abundance, or the notion that food could be plentiful. My idea of working as a sandwich hand was to put the same type of filling in between two slices of bread—the same type of bread—and that should be easy enough. It came as a shock to me, on my first day at the takeaway, that there existed such a vast variety of bread, numerous types of fillings and sauces and condiments to go with them, and the countless ways customers wanted to combine these ingredients to make their own filling.

I tried to learn by heart the names of an assortment of food on display on the hot food counter: dim sims, Chiko rolls, Four'n'Twenty meat pies, chicken schnitzel, salmon patties... These might be standard Australian takeaway fare, but I had never seen, heard of, nor tasted them before.

Standing behind the sandwich counter, I struggled to listen to a customer's lengthy order delivered in the typical Australian drawl, all in the same breath. It was impossible for me to remember what he wanted.

'Can I have a chicken sandwich in whole grain bread, please, with butter, not margarine... and... yes, with lettuce, onion, beetroot, carrot, salt and pepper, mustard... hmm... no, not mustard, sorry, I changed my mind, tomato sauce instead, and no salt and pepper.'

My concentration ability failed me after 'with butter, not margarine'.

It was lunch time. The workers in blue overalls from nearby factories started to flock into the takeaway, forming an impatient queue.

The male customer could see that not only was I lost, I was in panic. He kindly repeated the order, saying the name of each ingredient slowly, pointing it out for me one by one by placing his finger on the glass panel. It took me a long time to fill that order. The next one was not any simpler or shorter. I felt hot in the face, and not just because it was a warm day.

My Greek boss was serving customers at the deli counter. Now and then he threw me an impatient look.

My co-worker was also a Vietnamese refugee. She had been working here long before me. She could see I was struggling. I had been hired to assist her. Instead she had to take care of the hot food counter as well as my sandwich orders. I was completely useless.

It was clear that I would not last long in this job. The boss was kind but his brother was mean. One day I accidentally dropped a plastic straw on the floor.

The brother picked it up and waved it menacingly close to my face, grinding his teeth. 'You have just wasted a plastic straw.'

I felt angry, upset, and absolutely disappointed with myself. That was the end of my sandwich hand career.

A friend had been working as a waitress at a Chinese takeaway near where I lived. Her English class timetable clashed with her working hours at the takeaway. Her boss was happy for me to replace her.

Compared with the sandwich hand position, waiting tables was much easier. I simply took orders from customers and brought out the food. The owner of the takeaway, a Malaysian Chinese, was also the cook. His mother helped me clean the tables and do the dishes.

I could not ask for nicer bosses, however my pay was only three dollars an hour. I was happy to work there, but at the same time I was looking out for a better opportunity.

That opportunity came to me quite unexpectedly. My next job was much more interesting than making sandwiches and waiting tables.

A friend in English class told me that a welfare group called the Indo-Chinese Refugee Association was looking for a volunteer to help them translate a number of articles into Vietnamese for their bilingual newsletter. I told him right away that I was interested.

Since my disastrous experience as a sandwich hand, I had been dogged by nagging doubts about my ability to make something of myself in Australia. What good was I if I could not even prepare sandwiches!

I remembered the praise I received from my teachers and my friends for the essays and the stories I wrote for the school magazine, but what use was Vietnamese literature in this very English-speaking country? I felt depressed and quietly grieved for my wasted talent.

Now along came this translation job for a bilingual bulletin that provided handy information and advice to new migrants in Australia. What a terrific idea! I could put my ability in the Vietnamese language to good use and help my fellow refugees at the same time. This task was for me!

For several weeks, and a few hours each week, I went to ICRA's office in Melbourne CBD to work on the translations. Shelves bulging with thick files surrounded me. Paula, ICRA's coordinator, had been helping Indochinese refugees to settle in Australia. For those already here, she helped them fill out sponsorship applications so they could sponsor relatives who were still in refugee camps to come to Australia. Paula seemed to have a special affinity with the Vietnamese. She had adopted a pair of Vietnamese twin orphans, both of them blind.

I didn't realise that there were so many compassionate people like Paula in the world until I found myself among those in need. My experience as a refugee often made me ponder on the dark side of life and all the evils that human beings are capable of, things that caused me despair. It was people like Paula who brought me out of my sad thoughts and instilled in me a sense of hope.

One day a television producer rang Paula up. He asked her to help him find a young Vietnamese woman for a role in a popular Australian television series.

'You watch *Cop Shop*?' Paula asked me.

I didn't know *Cop Shop*, a hit police series at the time, from a bar of soap. I didn't watch much television. Colloquial English spoken in the fast and abbreviated way by the natives on television was just incomprehensible.

'No,' I said.

'It's a very big show here. I think you should give this a go,' Paula said.

Instead of feeling all excited at the prospect of appearing on television, I was hesitant, even embarrassed about it. Besides my pathological shyness, I had zero confidence in my looks. Acting had never been my aspiration.

'I don't think I'm at all photogenic, Paula,' I said.

'Well, there is no harm going to the audition. The pay is pretty good. A thousand or so for this role.'

A thousand or so? My student allowance was only forty dollars a week and my waitress job only paid three dollars an hour.

This was *a lot* of money.

I went to the Crawford Productions building in Richmond wearing a simple but pretty black dress bought specifically for the audition. An attractive lady came out to greet me and led me to her office. Her manner was particularly gentle and kind, perhaps because she knew I was a refugee. She asked for my height and weight, told me to stand without my shoes and gave me a quick glance from head to toe. She also asked me to read a few lines of conversation from a script. From her warm smile, I felt she had already made up her mind to give me this job.

'I don't think I am at all photogenic,' I said. I could not have been more unhelpful for my own cause.

'You'll be fine.' The lady smiled.

A work contract and pages of script were sent to Paula, who passed them on to me. My role was that of a recently arrived refugee, so I would simply play myself. I had to keep the script confidential until after all these episodes were broadcast.

I started learning the lines for my role.

There is a Vietnamese proverb: 'If you are deaf, the sound of gunfights won't scare you'. It described my present situation perfectly. I did not have a clue about what I was getting myself into, except for the fact that there would be a generous pay cheque made out in my name when this was all over. Had I possessed even a vague appreciation about what *real* acting required, perhaps I would have said no to the job to spare myself embarrassment, and to spare television viewers from having to put up with my poor attempt at acting.

My character did not speak English well and would be required to speak very little. This suited me perfectly.

I went back to the Crawford's building for rehearsal. When I arrived, a number of *Cop Shop* luminaries were already in the rehearsing room. It resembled an old classroom. People sat in old chairs in a semi-circle. Of course I did not know any of them or how famous they were, but, gee, were they all good looking! I politely greeted them with a nod, then quietly sat down, quietly read my lines when it was my turn, then quietly left when it was all finished. If acting had been my aspiration, this should have been my chance to mingle with the professionals and make myself noticed—but it never had been. It sounds bad saying it, but I only did this for money.

My first scene was shot in a back alley of an inner suburb with overgrown climbers hanging over dilapidated wooden fences. I had expected a film crew with all the impressive equipment—as in the movies—but the only piece of machinery

I could see was a hand-held video recorder. I felt slightly disappointed.

Had I realised what glamorous company I was with that day, I would have been totally bowled over and would have paid more notice to the stars than to the film equipment.

An elegant looking lady was particularly gentle and protective towards me. I felt drawn to her immediately. She had a slight frame and the graceful manner of a ballet dancer. Perhaps in her fifties, she was older than the rest of the crew. I could see they were very respectful towards her. I had the feeling she knew how out of place I felt and she made a point of giving me her special support. She explained to me, in her soft voice, what the scene was about and my role in it. I had not been given the script for this scene, perhaps because it was an action scene and all that I needed to do was to follow instructions.

This scene introduced me to the audience. I had just stolen an apple from a grocery shop and then fled into this alley. Two men from the shop chased me. They caught up with me, bashed me, then left me lying on the ground in pain, with blood running from my nose and red marks on my face. A policeman and a policewoman on routine patrol happened to go into the alley. They found me and rescued me.

Paula would later tell me that the elegant lady who directed this scene was Betty Pounder, a respected figure in the Australian arts scene. She was among *Cop Shop*'s team of directors. The policeman and the policewoman who rescued me were *Cop Shop* stars Gil Tucker and Lynda Stoner. Lynda Stoner was strikingly beautiful and voluptuous. She reminded me of Brigitte Bardot.

My last scene was shot at Channel Seven's studio in the city. When it was over, Gil, Lynda and a few people in the television crew took time to come and talk to me. The director allowed me to go into the production room to see all the television screens on the wall and the impressive control panels with hundreds of buttons on them. When it was time for me to leave, Lynda called a taxi for me.

Gil and Lynda might be big television stars but it was their kindness that made a strong impression on me. They treated me like a little sister. They understood how awkward I felt and went out of their way to make me feel more comfortable.

I admired Lynda even more when I found out, many years later, that like Brigitte Bardot, she was also an animal welfare activist.

Paula rang Betty Pounder to find out how I went. Apparently Betty was quite pleased with my performance. She later sent me a very encouraging letter that I cherished and still keep.

Shortly after my appearance on television, a little girl spotted me in the supermarket. She approached me and asked if I was in *Cop Shop*. She even had a pen and a piece of paper in her hands, ready for my autograph! I was not prepared for this kind of attention. I went red in the face, feeling totally embarrassed, instead of flattered, and to her disappointment, shyly shook my head and said, 'No.'

After a year in Australia, I still had trouble understanding the broad Aussie accent. No one in the street spoke English according to the Oxford Dictionary's phonetic instructions! Instead of 'Haauu… arre… you', they said 'H'ye'. Now, how could anyone work that out?

My classroom English, on the other hand, had improved a great deal. From introductory level, I soon progressed to intermediate, then advanced level.

At advanced level, the study materials were more challenging and interesting. The teacher gave each of us a copy of a poem titled 'Waltzing Matilda' by Banjo Paterson. He taught us to sing 'Waltzing Matilda', a song based on this poem. It was Australia's unofficial national anthem, he said. It told a tragic story of a 'swagman' who was caught stealing a 'jumbuck'. He ended his life by jumping into a 'billabong'.

We were also told about Australia's folk hero, Ned Kelly, an Australian version of Robin Hood, someone who stole from the rich to give to the poor.

My knowledge about Australian history was limited, but already I discerned a nation and a people with a benevolent disposition towards the luckless and the downtrodden. My family and I were among the lucky beneficiaries of that compassionate spirit. Australia had given us a second chance in life. I hoped I would be able to make the most out of it.

As my English improved, my taste in books became more sophisticated. From comics and children's books, I graduated to young adult series. With the help of a dictionary, I was determined to find the meaning and the correct pronunciation of every new word I came across. I read everything my eyes gazed upon, be it food labels, clothes labels, junk mail or the Bible. I hoped I had not committed blasphemy by using the holy book as an English learning tool. The Bible and a big framed picture of Jesus Christ, hung on the lounge room wall, were among the church's gifts to us.

The last intensive English course that prepared me for university was held at Footscray Institute of Technology (it is now Victoria University). I had been in Australia for a year now.

Jackie, the course coordinator, was a tall, charming lady in her late thirties. She always dressed elegantly and had a warm smile for her refugee students. None of us came to Australia with our parents. Even though we were of adult age, many of us often felt lost and lonely like young orphans in this new country. Jackie was happy to provide us with guidance and advice about anything and everything. She was our teacher, our counsellor, our mentor, and also our big and caring sister.

At the end of the course, Jackie held a separate talk with each of us to gauge our career aspirations.

Since I was little, I always wanted to be a writer. At school, Vietnamese literature had always been my best and favourite subject. As much as I trusted and respected Jackie, I kept this cherished dream to myself. Penning Vietnamese poems and novels in an English speaking country? It sounded absurd, even to me. Who would want to read it? Who would care about it?

I told Jackie of my 'revised' aspiration:

'I want to be a social worker.'

'And why do you want to be a social worker?' Jackie asked.

If I had been confident with my English, I would have provided her with a long answer, something like this:

I had a relatively privileged childhood. Being a refugee made me understand what it was like to be helpless and destitute. My survival, my life and death, depended totally on the mercy of strangers. It was a scary and precarious existence. From what I have gone through, I've realised that there are many people in the world who have to suffer and endure hardship through no fault of their own. I've also realised there are many kind-hearted people who do what they can to alleviate such hardship. I've received such kindness and hope that I can repay it, in some way, by helping others.

For now, a short answer was all I could manage:

'Because I want to help people.'

I was glad she did not laugh at me. I was still struggling to find my feet in this land and needed help myself. I was in no position to help anyone right now.

Jackie explained to me, in the kindest way, that while she acknowledged my good intentions, I did not yet possess the necessary skills to become a social worker. I would need to be fluent in English. I would need to possess a good understanding about Australian people, Australian society and its welfare system, among other things. My priority, she said, should be to choose a course that would give me the best chance to find employment, earn money and be independent. She was right, of course.

I had to put my dream to become a writer aside for now. If I was truly passionate about it, I told myself, I would find a way to realise it one day.

On enrolment day Jackie brought the refugee students – her brood – to Footscray Institute of Technology's administration office. It was only befitting that we enrolled in Poor Man's University, another name for this institution. It provided tertiary education to students from blue-collar suburbs.

The office hallway was crowded with prospective students. After picking up the enrolment forms, we followed Jackie to a quiet location away from the crowd so she could help us fill them in. Until this moment, many of us, myself included, were still not sure which course to enrol in.

As we were all in a bit of a panic, Jackie calmly told the girls to write down 'Accounting' in the 'Course applied' field, and for the boys, any branch of Engineering, be it Electrical, Mechanical, or Civil Engineering.

I duly followed her instructions, even though I had no idea what an Accounting course would entail. Without wanting to offend those who aspire to a career in accounting, frankly speaking, accounting had never been among what I had planned for my life, but I trusted Jackie instinctively and believed in her judgment. She was one of those rare and admirable people who truly cared for others. She certainly cared for us.

Looking back, I believe Jackie had purposefully left it until the very last minute to tell us which course we should enrol in, not because she wanted to put us through a last minute panic, but because she had our best interests at heart. At the time none of us was informed enough to make this decision for ourselves. Jackie must have thought so, through her one-on-one talks with each of us. My unrealistic aspiration to become a social worker, out of a vague desire 'to do good', was a case in point. Another girl wanted to be a policewoman. Another one wanted to work for the United Nations. Our dreams seemed to stem from our refugee experience. We had suffered hardship and injustice. Some of us wanted to redress what went wrong with the world. Like a parent who knows best, Jackie had already made that important career decision for us, and wisely left it till the last minute so we did not have the chance to argue back and forth about something of which we had no clear understanding.

Now that I had just signed up for a course I had no interest in nor aptitude for, I just had to trudge through it. Mathematics was my least favourite school subject. I had never been able to relate to it. Figures did not excite me. I admired the Maths geniuses in the world because they understood all those complicated formulas that only gave me a headache. I was like a fish forced to learn how to fly, or a bird to swim. Often I felt overwhelmed and resented my life as a refugee, being thrown into alien territory and having to struggle with all my might, against my inherent tendency and natural ability, in order to survive.

Poring over tomes of thick, heavy textbooks full of jargon and complicated concepts written in a foreign language was torture.

I would love to say that my positive attitude had got me through the course. The truth was I was driven by fear – palm sweating, heart trembling, doom awaiting, naked fear. Fear of failure, fear of humiliation, fear of disappointing my parents who had sacrificed so much and risked everything to save their children from a hopeless life under communism. I was also fearful of disappointing myself if I failed to seize the chance Australia had given me to start my life anew. I wanted to rise up from the bottom of Australian society to where I had been, a young woman sure of her ability and her future. I was desperate to reclaim my pride.

Assignments were normally handed out at the beginning of each term. I started on them straight away and proceeded at my snail pace. I would consult the dictionary relentlessly and would often borrow half a dozen reference books for my one page essay. Even then I was still unsure whether my answer made enough sense. The assignment that took me a couple of months to complete, some Aussie students holed themselves up in the library cubicles to work on it the day it was due. If I needed a shock reminder as to how far behind I was and how exceptionally hard I had to work to catch up with everybody else, this was it.

I duly went to lectures, but understanding what the lecturer said was a totally different matter. I felt grateful whenever handouts were given. Often the lecturer would just drone on and on. I gave up any pretention that I could follow what he was saying. Instead I would frantically jot down in my notebook anything I could discern from his scribble on the whiteboard, or whatever was shown on the overhead projector screen. I would shamelessly peek at the notes taken by the person sitting next to me and copy them down. Often he or she would be kind enough to let me do that, except for one mean girl who did not want to help me. She covered her notes with her palms.

University often meant freedom, self-affirmation and self-growth. It was not just a place to impart and foster knowledge. Free from high school discipline, it often was a place for young adults bursting with energy to socialise, explore, take part in all sorts of activities because they wanted to and not because they had to: music, sports, political debate, and yes, sexual experiments would also be high on the list. Through all that, hopefully they would learn more about themselves and the world, and gain a better idea about where they stood in the scheme of things.

Unfortunately I do not have any fond memories about university to reminisce on. I was an outsider hovering at the fringe of university community life; my nagging fear was to be kicked out of it altogether.

I did not dare open my mouth even once in any lecture or tutorial session. I was afraid I could not make myself understood and would make a fool of myself. I had two classmates for support: Penny, a Laotian refugee, and Hang, another Vietnamese refugee. We shared notes, helped each other with assignments, sometimes we even lent each other money. A couple of Australian students said hello to me, but something prevented me from befriending them, something deep and painful that I would rather not spell out: my lack of confidence, my inferiority complex, my hurt pride. I suspected those young Aussies who reached out to me only did so out of pity. I did not want anyone to pity me. I had never been a subject of pity before.

I remembered the types of kids who attracted this kind of well-meaning but condescending attitude from the teachers and their peers at my school in Vietnam: someone with a handicap, someone who was sweet-natured but not too bright, someone who turned up at school wearing a uniform that clearly had seen better days and shoes that did not quite fit. Someone who stood out for the worst possible reasons. Now, on an Australian university campus, I was that someone.

I had been guilty of displaying well-meaning condescension towards my less fortunate schoolmates without any idea how this would make them feel. Now I knew. They must have felt like crying.

There existed a huge invisible wall between me and the Aussie students. They were outgoing and confident; they joked and laughed loudly as though they did not have a care in the world. How could they understand me and the world that I came from, a world of senseless cruelty and devastation, of immense suffering and loss. I was still reeling from what I had been through. No, it was not their fault we had not yet found common ground.

It astounded me that the Aussie students were allowed to consume food, drinks, and even chew gum in class. They showed no fear towards the lecturers. They asked questions, argued their points, voiced their opinions confidently .

In South Vietnam before the Communist upheavals, there was a clear hierarchical divide between student and teacher. As teachers were tasked with the important mission of imparting knowledge and wisdom, following the Confucian code of conduct, students were supposed to treat them with utmost respect. If ever they wanted to question them or contradict them, they needed to be ever so tactful so as not to cause the teachers to feel their authority was challenged. Vietnamese students certainly did not eat, drink or chew gum in class!

My family lived in Ascot Vale for eighteen months before moving to a high-rise housing commission flat in Carlton. Father Smith and Karen, of St John's parish in East Melbourne, had applied for public housing for us.

I truly do not know how we could ever manage to muddle through our early years in Australia without the help of so many kind-hearted people from the Catholic Church.

Almost without exception, in Australia as in other countries in the world, it was the Christian Churches—Catholic, Baptist, Protestant, Anglican, Presbyterian and Lutheran—that rallied their congregations to help Vietnamese refugees settle in their new homelands.

Reverend Father Kevin Smith, my family's benefactor, was a legend at St John's church. He passed away in 1995. At his funeral, an empty purse was placed on top of his coffin. This summed up his charitable attitude to life. He would rather give a few 'bucks' to nine cheaters in order not to miss a genuine one.[48] The Vietnamese Communists' motto was similar to Father Smith's, with a slight variance. They would rather kill nine innocent people in order not to miss the one they were after.

Father Smith was a tall, distinguished man with a booming voice and a generous smile. I learned to make tea for him the Australian way, with fresh milk and one sugar. I also learned to make coffee for Karen the Australian way, with fresh milk and no sugar. Fresh milk was a luxury to us. In Vietnam we only had sweetened condensed milk. Having tea or coffee with fresh milk was unheard-of luxury. White coffee made the Vietnamese way was, in fact, black coffee with a dollop of sweetened condensed milk, giving it a really sugary taste. Karen had quite a surprise when she asked for a cup of white coffee and was given this Vietnamese version. I, on the other hand, was surprised that she did not want any sugar in her coffee. In Communist Vietnam we rarely saw sugar in our rations and craved for it. Here in Australia, sugar was plentiful, yet Karen did not want any. No wonder human beings are rarely happy. We tend not to appreciate what we have and vie for something that is out of our reach.

Karen said Carlton, the Melbourne suburb that my family would be moving to, was very posh. She explained 'posh' meant very stylish and elegant. She might have been referring to another part of Carlton, not the high-rise purposefully built for the poor and the underprivileged that would be our new abode, but wanted to make us feel good about it. In any case I was unaware of the general stigma attached to public housing. I simply felt excited about this good news. From drifting at sea for days in a rickety boat to sleeping on wooden plank in a refugee camp, Midway migrant hostel had already been a huge improvement in housing standards for me. I opened my heart to Australian life without prejudgment or prejudice, and found every new experience and situation equally refreshing and exciting.

The high-rise in Carlton had a lot of positive attributes. It was only a two-minute walk to the prestigious Melbourne University. My clever little sister Linh had been doing very well at high school. There was every reason to believe she would find a place there. Fashion shops and popular restaurants lined the streets nearby. Those expensive places were beyond our means, but nothing prevented Linh and me giving ourselves the occasional treat of gelati and some mouth-watering Italian pastry from Brunetti's. The charming green city tram stopped right in front of our building. Families with children might prefer a place with plenty of open space, sunshine and nature, but for single adults like us, this location was perfect. The sometimes stinking lift and the occasional theft of our clothes from the communal laundry seemed to be the only setbacks.

Our flat was at one end of the fourteenth floor. Our neighbour, an Australian lady in her fifties, greeted us warmly and made us feel welcome right away. She loved plants and flowers. We were the gratuitous beneficiaries of her passion. Her many flower pots lined the plain walls of the corridor, transforming our concrete surroundings into a place imbued with life and colour.

I regret not remembering her name. She always dressed well and wore subtle make-up, her blond hair usually set in a stylish perm. She told me she once owned a nice house in a nice suburb, but since her husband died she had fallen on hard times. Her arthritic fingers with the nails painted bright red looked painfully twisted, but she never talked about her illness. She lived alone. I noticed that in the three years we lived next door to her, her only son, a man in his thirties, came to visit her exactly three times; this always occurred on Mother's Day. On those special days she would go into town in the morning to get her hair done. Back from the hairdresser, she would dress up and get herself ready well before her son arrived. He would always come with a nice bunch of flowers in his hand, and mother and son would go somewhere to celebrate. She seemed both happy and nervous in his company, happy to see him again, nervous—I guessed—because she knew the happy moment would not last and she would be returning to her lonely existence again when he had gone.

It occurred to me that in the long interval between her son's visits, my family might be the only people she spoke to every day.

She did not seem to be bothered by that. Perhaps she had been used to that, and yet I could not help feeling a bit sad for her.

We were her neighbours on the right. Her neighbour on the left was also a middle-aged woman who lived alone. I never saw the two women talk to each other. I never saw the other woman venture outside her flat either. She did not seem to have any visitors. I tended to throw a quick and curious glance through the sheer curtain of her kitchen window whenever I walked past. Almost always I would see her slumping in front of the television, thick rolls of fat banded around her huge body that bulged uncomfortably under her calf-length nightgown.

My glimpse into the lives of these women had given me a hint of the bleak side of Australian society: the deterioration of human interaction, the lack of strong family ties, the isolation and loneliness experienced by many, and the problem that often besets people of a rich country—obesity. As material affluence brought about self-sufficiency, it had also eaten away a sense of community.

Living in this public housing commission flat gave me a sober view about Australia as a society. The glamorous and romantic images of the Western world and its people, as projected in Hollywood movies, had quietly dissipated in me. I could see the majority of people in the street did not look like or dress like movie stars. Ordinary Australians seemed to be no different to ordinary Vietnamese; no one escaped the mandatory participation in the maddening rat race, everyone had to rush to work to earn a living in the morning, come home in the afternoon slightly disheveled and depleted, then start the same thing all over again the next, and the next day.

Those who lived in housing commission flats were either Australians down on their luck, like our neighbours, or migrants and refugees like us, who also struggled, but aspired to a better life. Those who had acquiesced to their unlucky fate possessed a humble bearing, dressed impeccably in the fashion of an indecipherable era carefully selected from a nearby Vinnies community shop. They deserved some dignity, just for that effort alone. Then there were those who seemed to have given up on life. They no longer cared about their appearance. Every time I saw them, they still wore the same clothes that smelled like sweat, dampness, stale wine, cigarettes, or a mixture of all of those things. They had the bearing of someone who was in a permanent daze; through their prism the world was nothing but a deeply unsatisfactory and confusing mess. Some young girls from the housing commission hung around the tram stop all day. They waited for passengers to alight then approached them asking for money or cigarettes.

The tragedy of poverty, no matter where it struck, in a housing commission in Melbourne or a shanty town in Saigon, left the same imprint on the face of its victims—the face of a perpetual worrier: eyes clouded by past, current or pending financial or health disasters; permanent expression of bewilderment, bitterness, resignation, sadness and powerlessness at the injustice that seemed to stack against them, the question—'Why me?'—never satisfactorily answered. It was deeply worrying that, for some of them, the bleak thought of relinquishing all hopes and aspirations seemed to be a sensible option.

And, as in the alleyways of Saigon, in the small streets of Carlton there were urine stains on the walls and rubbish strewn on the ground too.

There was another Vietnamese refugee family living on our floor. Tan, the husband, worked night shift in a bread factory. The couple had a young son. They invited us over for lunch. That was the start of our friendship.

Often, past midnight, we would hear a hurried knock at the door together with Tan's happy announcement even before we went to answer it:

'Energy supplies for my little brother and sisters, so you can study super hard!' Free bread and croissants were the perks of his job. He always filled up one bag for his family and one for us before clocking off, and dashed to our flat to give it to us before heading home. The bread and the croissants, from the night's latest batch, were still warm. He knew that in those wee hours of the night we were still poring over our textbooks.

Tan came from a very wealthy family in Saigon. He often talked about his family's sprawling property, as big as a golf course, which was confiscated by the Communists. He possessed the confidence and assertiveness of a go-getter, someone who was used to being in charge. His Aussie boss had benefited from his credentials. With a degree in Economics and years in management positions in South Vietnam when our country was still free, Tan was more than qualified in giving his boss good suggestions on how to improve productivity. He was promoted to the position of supervisor after a short stint as a factory hand. His wife was a sweet-looking lady with a soft voice and a gentle manner. She was as calm and delicate as he was bold and boisterous.

He was absolutely appalled when he caught sight of my brother Tin doing the dishes or returning from the shops with heavy shopping bags:

'How come you do the dishes? How come you do the shopping? Come on, you are a gentleman. Leave housework to the women!'

He had already won us over with his warm nature and kindheartedness. We were willing to overlook his prejudice and just laughed it off. Some people possess that kind of charm.

The calamity brought about by a change of government in Vietnam had drastically altered his social status. The fact that this scion of a notable family in South Vietnam had to work in a bread factory and live in a housing commission flat, starting his life all over again from the bottom of Australian society, did not seem to faze him. He was sure of his worth, confident of his potential, and decided that the disparity between the circumstances he found himself in and his rightful place in the world was only temporary. Already he talked about amassing enough savings to invest in business ventures and properties.

He cited the names of Melbourne suburbs with the highest capital growth. I don't know how he obtained such up-to-date investment information.

Tan's family moved out of the housing commission before us. A few years later, we were not at all surprised to hear he had become the successful owner of a milk bar and his family had settled in a nice suburb.

His was the kind of success that made all Vietnamese refugees proud.

The year 1982, four years after my family arrived to Australia, was a milestone year for us.

I was in my last year of an Accounting degree. My brother Tin was also in his last year of a Computing degree. My little sister Linh was finishing Year 12. She would be among the top performers in that year's Higher School Certificate (HSC) examinations. Our single-mindedness towards one goal, and one goal only—study, study and study—had borne fruit. Both my sister Ba and my stepsister My secured employment as interpreters.

It was during the semester break of 1982 that I received a letter from Telecom Australia (now Telstra) calling me for an interview. I had sat for a recruitment test in December the previous year, but had not heard anything from them since. I had presumed I did not pass. This letter was good news. I had been living on the poverty line long enough. This was my chance to earn some decent income. I was getting sick of having jam sandwiches that I prepared from home and brought to university every day for lunch, when other students enjoyed hot meals at the canteen. I did not try the snacks vending machines even once; my budget did not allow such indulgence. At university I always drank tap water, but did give myself permission for chilled fruit drinks in the hot months of the sweltering Australian summer.

From my well-paid role in *Cop Shop*, I had managed to put aside some money for a rainy day. I spent it on my interview outfit: a nice dress, a nice jacket and a decent pair of high heels.

In the interview, I was asked why I had applied for the job.

'For financial reasons. I would like to earn some money,' I politely answered, as innocent as a lamb.

I did not have any job interview training and was absolutely ignorant about what to say and what not to say in an interview. I was simply being honest.

The male and the female interviewers looked at each other, then asked me to wait while they went outside to talk to each other.

A short while later, the gentleman came back and told me, 'You've got the job.'

I had no idea whether it was because I was the best candidate or because they felt sorry for me.

I decided to take up the offer, work full-time and study the remaining subjects of my university course part-time. My bank balance improved right away. That kept me with Telecom for a while.

The good news kept coming. A couple of months after my start with Telecom, I received a letter from Footscray Institute of Technology informing me I had been awarded a scholarship worth five hundred dollars, a princely sum, for having achieved high distinctions in two Statistics subjects. These were the subjects that I loathed the most, feared to fail the most, and so had spent the most time and shed the most tears on them. I would have been relieved just to pass; never in my wildest dreams would I have thought that I would achieve these top results.

My record of always finishing a school year with a prize, to my great surprise, had been maintained. Confusingly, I did not feel at all exuberant. Rather, I felt like the tortoise that had finally reached the finishing line in its race against the hare — absolutely miserable and exhausted. Having had to participate in an unequal match, having been forced to spend down to the very last ounce of its energy, all it wanted to do was collapse on the ground for a momentary respite. The applaud of race spectators that erupted following its unlikely feat sounded unreal and remote, as though it came from a dream. It failed to register with the poor animal. Every muscle in its body was aching. It was busy tending its wounds. Already it was thinking of challenges ahead. Life would not suddenly become easy after this win. Its disadvantages were inherent. It would still have to deal with them for the rest of its life.

Yes, that was the reason for my rather subdued reaction to the good news. The challenges and the disadvantages associated with being a new migrant in a new land would still persist; I would still face them every day. The award was an encouraging pat on my back, but I still had many mountains to climb.

I decided not to make a big deal out of it. I was allowed to bring guests to the award ceremony and could have asked my siblings to come along, but decided not to. It was more important for them not to miss school and work.

The ceremony was on a Tuesday. I chose a nice dress for the occasion, went to work as usual, but clocked off early for the day. I took a bus from where I worked to the university where the ceremony was held.

The reception hall was packed with smartly-dressed and important-looking people, representatives of prize donors from various industries and businesses. If I were a savvy self-promoter, as new university graduates were encouraged to be, this could be my chance to mingle, introduce myself, exchange business cards and make small talk with those who could further my career.

However I was still a shy girl from a far away mountain city in the Central Highlands of South Vietnam; a refugee still grappling with the Australian culture; a new migrant not yet confident in her grasp of English, still afraid she would embarrass herself in front of everyone.

As always, whenever I was unsure about what I was supposed to do, I felt nervous and slightly panicked. I discreetly headed to a relatively quiet corner away from the food and drinks tables where most people gathered and hid myself there.

The ceremony started with short speeches from the school dignitaries before the names of prize recipients were called.

A professor took on the role of compere for the occasion. He paused for a second, explaining himself to the audience in a light-hearted manner before calling my name:

'Hmm… I'm not quite sure how to pronounce the next student's name, but I will give it a go anyway… K w o a n … or Kwi… Dao?'

There were well-meaning chuckles in the audience. I walked to the podium with an embarrassed smile on my face.

Four years before, I arrived in Australia with little English and little confidence in myself. My dream of finishing university had seemed out of reach. I did not know what to do with my life.

Now the future did not seem so scary. There might be bigger goals to reach, higher mountains to climb, but for now I was happy with what I had achieved so far. My hard work had paid off.

A gentleman handed me an envelope with my prize in it.

'Well done,' he said.

I thanked him profusely. A surge of pride warmed my heart. I wished my parents were here to share with me this special moment.

It was only a short walk from where I sat to the podium to receive my prize amid a clapping of hands and smiles of encouragement from the audience, but for me it had been such a long and arduous personal journey.

The Beauty That Remains

With our friends at Midway Hostel (Melbourne, Australia, 1979)
Left to right: My niece in a friend's lap, me, little sister
Linh, sister Ba, brother Tin, a friend, brother Chau.

With my English class at Midway Hostel
(sitting down third from right, 1979)

Quynh Dao

With my little sister Linh at Carlton public housing flat, Melbourne (1981)

Ba, Tin, My (standing left to right) and Linh, Melbourne (1982)

The Beauty That Remains

Melbourne (1982)

With my parents and my
son, Melbourne (2000)

EPILOGUE

November 2010
It is a warm, beautiful spring day. My son and I are on a city-bound tram to Melbourne Town Hall to attend a special ceremony celebrating thirty-five years of Vietnamese settlement in Australia. Following the Communist victory in 1975, approximately 90,000 Vietnamese refugees were granted permanent settlement in Australia. There are now over 180,000 Australians of Vietnamese background.

It seems only yesterday when I was a teenager gripped with anxiety, not knowing what the future held for me when I first came to Australia.

How time flies.

I am now a fifty-year-old woman who feels she now earns the right to look back on her life and reminisce. I have earned the right to start my sentences with 'in my younger years', or 'when I was your age', when giving my son life lessons, as old parents often do. My sweet son often shakes his head and looks at me with a lot of love in his eyes, saying 'Mum, I cannot believe that you have been through so much!' He rolls his eyes in exasperation when I insist, at times with a forcefulness that borders on irrationality, that he should finish his meal and not throw the still edible food in the bin. There are starving people in refugee camps who would love to have that bit of leftover, I say to him. When my son detects my reluctance at throwing away any food past its use-by date, he labels it 'the refugee camp syndrome'. No doubt my refugee camp experience has left an imprint on me, on the way I view the world. It sometimes causes me to suddenly become intense and emotional over something to which my son would respond, quite rightly, 'Mum, what's wrong? What's the big deal?'

I still feel infinitely sad when I look at the sea. It reminds me of my escape journey and over half a million Vietnamese who did not make it. The sea is their eternal resting place. I'm not going to make any excuse for that feeling. I think, subjectively of course, that having gone through a life-shattering experience, one is entitled to be a bit cranky, a bit unhinged, a bit mad. That is the way my delightful son sometimes endearingly and humorously describes me.

I finished my Accounting degree and have been working in the field for over twenty-five years now. I still dislike figures and remain a reluctant accountant, a profession I was enlisted into by an accident of fate. However it helped me obtain a secure job, freed me from financial worries, and allows me to indulge in my literary passion, penning stories and poems in my spare time.

My stepsister My moved to the United States. She is now a broadcaster for Voice of America. My sister Ba enjoys doing research. She obtained a PhD in information technology. My stepbrother and my brothers all work in the computing field. Tin is a successful IT executive. My little sister Linh achieved top result in her Higher School Certificate (HSC) exam as predicted and gained entry to University of Melbourne School of Medicine. She tragically passed away while in her second year. I don't think I can ever get over the fact that my baby sister is no longer with me.

After ten years of separation, in 1989, my parents were allowed to leave Vietnam to reunite with their children in Australia.

Since 1986, Vietnam started economic reforms and opened its door to the world, however there has been no change to the Vietnamese Communist Party's monopoly on political power. It is now 2016. The Vietnamese people are still not free. The government still responds to peaceful demands for freedom and democracy with brutality. The Socialist Republic of Vietnam remains 'socialist' only in name. Emeritus Professor of History Pierre Brocheux described post-socialist Vietnam as a society 'restructured according to a monetary hierarchy, leading to a growing inequality of income and social status'.[49]

Among the most scathing critics of the communist system nowadays are veteran communists, who see their country falling further and further into a dead end of poverty and hopelessness.

Among the greatest defenders of South Vietnam nowadays are the young generation who trust the internet more than Party propaganda. They read about a fledgling democracy that thrived and achieved so much, about the freedom that South Vietnamese enjoyed, even in time of war. Many question, some reject outright, the well-worn official triumphalism version of the war.

Lawyer Nguyen Van Dai was six years old when the war ended. He is now a well known human rights and democracy advocate. In 2013, on the occasion of the 38th anniversary of the communist victory, he said:

'A nation had achieved independence and reunification, yet its people still do not enjoy basic freedoms, democracy and human rights; this means that they had shed their blood and sacrificed their lives in vain. They had fought against foreign oppressors, not to have it replaced by oppressors from within. Damnably, the oppressors within – the Party leadership - are one hundred times, one thousand times greedier and more brutal than the foreign enemy.

'My thoughts and feelings about this fateful day? I feel sad and regretful. A democratic system of government lost to a brutal one-party dictatorship, civilisation lost to barbarity. Evil had triumphed.'[50]

Vietnam's attitude towards former refugees who now belong to a successful diaspora in the West is ambivalent. They possess an important source of foreign capital and brain power much needed for nation building. However, they are also living witnesses of an inhumane political system and reminders of a tragic period in Vietnamese history that the authorities want to erase.

There are now approximately four million Vietnamese living abroad in over one hundred countries around the world. The majority of them are former refugees and their descendants. Their sentimental attachment to their former homeland is now keenly evoked in emotive language. The erstwhile 'traitors' and 'scum of the earth' are now referred to, rather flatteringly, as 'our flesh and blood from far away lands'.

At the same time, Vietnam puts pressure on governments of neighbouring countries, such as Indonesia and Malaysia, to destroy memorials erected in these countries to commemorate those who died in the exodus. There are makeshift cemeteries in Pulau Galang in Indonesia, Pulau Bidong in Malaysia and in several other locations along the coastlines of Southeast Asia, where bodies of refugees that washed ashore were buried. Van Kho Thuyen Nhan Viet Nam (Archive of Vietnamese Boat People) has taken on the admirable task of finding and reconstructing these cemeteries to give the deceased a decent resting place.

'Mum, what are you thinking? Are you nervous?' My son nudges my elbow, pulling me back to reality.

The launching of my first book, a memoir titled *Tales from a Mountain City*, is a part of today's ceremony. I will be giving a short speech. My son knows that I have been fretting about it in the last few days.

My dream of being a writer has never left me. It took me eight years to finish *Tales from a Mountain City*. Writing in a second language is a challenge. English grammar is a nightmare. I wrestled with every word and every sentence. I received several rejections but never gave up. I believe that the story of three generations of my family in the tumultuous context of the Vietnam War is a story that deserves to be told. The day I received a publishing offer was among the best days of my life.

And here I am, standing on the podium in a packed room of Melbourne Town Hall, feeling both nervous and elated. Former Prime Minister Malcolm Fraser, the Vietnamese refugees' great benefactor, and his wife Tamie, sit in the front row. They are today's ceremony's guests of honour. Many among the audience hold a copy of my book in their hands, some impatiently flipping through it, some already poring over the first few pages. I am living my dream.

I tell the audience about a refugee girl who had been given a second chance in life. I thank the compassionate people of a beautiful land called Australia who had given me the precious gift of freedom and the opportunity to fulfill my potential.

From where he stands, my son looks at me adoringly and gives me the biggest smile that melts my heart. My child has grown up to be a happy, positive and talented young man. He is my rock, my best friend and my number one fan. He is an Aussie through and through, who loves watching football and placing a bet on a horse race, but is also very proud of his Vietnamese cultural heritage. I can't ask for a better son.

My dear son, you have the chance to live in a free and humane society, so you are luckier than most people. You can be all that you want to be, and do all that you want to do in life. Cherish what you have and embrace life for all its wonders.

There may be challenges along life's path that, at times, seem insurmountable; there may be times when you feel like the world is crashing down on you; instances when you feel as though the pain in your heart is just too great to bear. Believe me when I tell you I have been through all that.

But take heart. Be patient. Believe also when I tell you that there is enough sunshine to warm your heart, enough love and compassion in this world to make up for your sadness, and enough simple pleasures to bring joy back to your life.

Follow what is dearest to your heart, because dreams can come true.

ACKNOWLEDGMENTS

I'd like to thank Tom Flood for his subtle and concise editing.

My grateful thanks to Mrs Tamie Fraser and Most Reverend Vincent Long for kindly and generously taking the time from their busy schedules to provide the introduction and the foreword.

The Vietnamese refugee community in Australia is forever indebted to Mrs Fraser and her husband, the late former Prime Minister of Australia Malcolm Fraser, for their most heart-warming care and compassion.

My thanks to Hung Chau, Vivienne Nguyen and Claudia Nguyen of the Vietnamese Community in Australia (Victoria Chapter) for their support for my book.

My big thanks to my brother, my sister and my stepsister for their anecdotes.

My mother and my son are my staunchest supporters in everything I do. My son is my first reader, editor and fabulous - obviously unbiased - reviewer. Thank you for being the rock of my life.

ABOUT THE AUTHOR

Quynh Dao escaped Vietnam by boat to Malaysia and came to Australia as a refugee in 1979. She is a member of Amnesty International.

Her first book *Tales from a Mountain City* was shortlisted for the Asher Literary Award in 2011 and the William Saroyan International Prize for Writing in 2012.

The Beauty That Remains was shortlisted for the Finch Memoir Prize in 2014.

NOTES

1. M. P. Royan, Letter to the Editor, *Herald Malaysia* online, 16 March 2009.
2. Jacqueline Desbarats, 'Repression in the Socialist Republic of Vietnam: Execution and Population Relocation' in *The Vietnam Debate*, ed. John Norton Moore, University Press of America, 1990, pp. 196-197; see also Nathalie Huynh Chau Nguyen, *Memory Is Another Country – Women of the Vietnamese Diaspora*, Praeger, 2009, p. 30, note 16 for additional sources.
3. Dang Phong, *Lich Su Kinh Te Viet Nam 1945-2000, Tap II: 1955-1975 (Vietnam's Economic History, 1945–2000, Vol. 2.: 1955-1975)*, Vietnam Academy of Social Science, Social Science Publishing House (NXB Khoa học Xã hội), 2005, p. 5.
4. Pierre Brocheux, *Ho Chi Minh: A Biography*, p. 152.
5. BBC Vietnamese online, 'A rare conversation with Huu Loan', 5 and 12 October 2002. _____, 'A tribute to the poet Huu Loan', 20 March 2010.
6. Kim Huynh, *Where the Sea Takes Us*, Fourth Estate, 2007, p. 291.
7. *Chosun Ilbo* online, 'Korean Who Rescued Vietnamese Boat People Not Forgotten', 6 August 2004.
8. *Los Angeles Times* online, 'Boat People Celebrate Rescuer - Eighteen years after he saved 96 people, a South Korean fisherman is thanked in grand style', 9 August 2004.
9. Hal G. P. Colebatch, 'The Left Rewrites Its History on Refugees', *Quadrant* online, October 2010 – Volume LIV Number 10.
10. Viktor E. Frankl, *Man's Search for Meaning*, Rider, 2008, p. 109.

11. Kim Huynh, *Where the Sea Takes Us*, pp. 299, 307-308.
12. Malcolm Fraser and Margaret Simmons, *Malcolm Fraser The Political Memoirs*, The Miegunyah Press, 2010, p. 744.
13. Larry Englemann, 'Joe Devlin, The Boat People's Priest', published online 12 June 2006, http://www.historynet.com/joe-devlin-the-boat-peoples-priest.htm, [viewed 15 September 2016].
14. Viktor E. Frankl, *Man's Search for Meaning*, p. 76.
15. Huy Duc, *Ben Thang Cuoc*, Osin Book, 2012, p. 230.
16. Huy Duc, p. 238.
17. Huy Duc, pp. 238-240 .
18. Huy Duc, p. 238.
19. Huy Duc, p. 239.
20. ibid.
21. Huy Duc, p. 369.
22. Huy Duc, pp. 74, 181-182.
23. Huy Duc, p. 376.
24. Gerard Henderson, 'Thirty years on, an occasion for some to say sorry', *The Sydney Morning Herald*, 26 April 2005.
25. Clyde Cameron, *China, Communism and Coca-Cola*, Hill of Content, 1980, p. 228.
26. Hal G. P. Colebatch, 'The Left Rewrites Its History on Refugees'.
27. Clyde Cameron, *China, Communism and Coca-Cola*, p. 230.
28. Gerard Henderson, 'The Whitlam Government & Indo-Chinese Refugees', *The Sydney Institute Quarterly*, Issue 19, Vol. 7 No. 1 March 2003, p. 18.
29. Lloyd Duong, *Boat People: Imprints on History*, Part III International Responses to the Boat People Tragedy, Canada Digital Collections, 2000, p. 13.
30. Jane Fonda, *My Life So Far*, Random House, 2005, p. 356.
31. *The Milwaukee Sentinel*, 'Joan Baez, Jane Fonda duel over Vietnam', 3 July 1979.
32. Michel Winock, 'Sartre s'est-il toujours trompe?', first published in *L'Histoire*, Issue 295, February 2005, http://www.diplomatie.gouv.fr/fr/IMG/pdf/0203-Winock-FR-5.pdf, [viewed 15 September 2016]; see also Lloyd Duong, *Boat People: Imprints on History*, p. 58.

33. Benedict O'Donohoe, 'Why Sartre Matters', *Philosophy Now*, Sartre centenary issue, Issue 53 November / December 2005, https://philosophynow.org/issues/53/Why_Sartre_Matters [viewed 15 September 2016].
34. Lloyd Duong, *Boat People: Imprints on History*, p. 58.
35. Alexander Solzhenitsyn, Harvard University Address, Thursday 8 June 1978, http://www.orthodoxytoday.org/articles/SolzhenitsynHarvard.php [viewed 15 September 2016].
36. Pierre Brocheux, *Ho Chi Minh: A Biography*, p. 175.
37. Huy Duc, *Ben Thang Cuoc*, p. 283.
38. Qiang Zhai, *China and the Vietnam Wars, 1950-1975*, The University of North Carolina Press, 2000, pp. 135, 220.
39. Huy Duc, *Ben Thang Cuoc*, p. 112.
40. Qiang Zhai, *China and the Vietnam Wars*, p. 217.
41. ibid.
42. Voice of Russia Vietnamese online, *Nhin Lai Ngay Hom Qua series (Reminiscing the Past 65 years of Russia-Vietnam cooperation)*, 22 December 2014, http://vietnamese.ruvr.ru/2014_12_22/281577198/ [viewed 15 September 2016]; see also http://vietnamese.ruvr.ru/tag_80492902/ [viewed 15 September 2016].
43. Qiang Zhai, *China and the Vietnam Wars*, p. 214.
44. Vu Thu Hien, *Dem Giua Ban Ngay (Nightfall in the Middle of the Day)*, Van Nghe, 1997, p 422; see also RFA Vietnamese online, 'Giai Phong Mien Nam: Cho Ai va Vi ai?' (Liberating South Vietnam: For Whom and For What?), Part 2, 29 April 2011.
45. Voice of Russia Vietnamese online, 'Cung chung suc chong cuoc tan cong tu phuong Bac' (Join force to counter the attack from the North), 15 January 2015, http://vietnamese.ruvr.ru/2015_01_15/282129227/ [viewed 15 September 2016].
46. Malcolm Fraser and Margaret Simmons, *Malcolm Fraser The Political Memoirs*, pp. 276-277.
47. Trinh Xuan Thuan, 'Science and Buddhism', published online 2010, *Universite Interdisciplinaire de Paris*, http://uip.edu/en/articles-en/science-and-buddhism, [viewed 15 September 2016].
48. Catholic Archdiocese of Melbourne/ Saint Patrick's Cathedral/ History/ St John The Evangelist, East Melbourne, The Legends of

St John's, http://www.cam.org.au/cathedral/History/Saint-John-the-Evangelist-East-Melbourne, [viewed 15 September 2016].
49. Pierre Brocheux, *Ho Chi Minh: A Biography*, p. 186.
50. Nguyen Van Dai, 'Neu Viet Nam Cong Hoa chien thang?' ('How different our nation could have turned out to be if the Republic of South Vietnam had won the war?'), BBC online, 29 April 2013.

BIBLIOGRAPHY

Berman, Larry, *No Peace, No Honour – Nixon, Kissinger, and Betrayal in Vietnam*, Simon & Schuster, New York, 2002.

Brocheux, Pierre, *Ho Chi Minh: A Biography*, Cambridge University Press, 2007.

Cameron, Clyde, *China, Communism and Coca-Cola*, Hill of Content, 1980.

Colebatch, Hal G. P., 'The Left Rewrites Its History on Refugees', *Quadrant* online, Volume LIV Number 10, October 2010.

Dao, Quynh, *Tales from a Mountain City*, Odyssey Books, 2010.

Duong, Lloyd, *Boat People: Imprints on History*, Canada Digital Collections, 2000.

Fonda, Jane, *My Life So Far*, Random House, 2005.

Frankl, Viktor E., *Man's Search for Meaning*, Rider, 2008.

Fraser, Malcolm and Simmons, Margaret, *Malcolm Fraser The Political Memoirs*, The Miegunyah Press, 2010.

Henderson, Gerard, 'The Whitlam Government & Indo-Chinese Refugees', *The Sydney Institute Quarterly*, Issue 19, Vol. 7 No. 1 March 2003.

Huy Duc, *Ben Thang Cuoc (The Winning Side)* Part I, OsinBook, 2012.

Huynh, Kim, *Where the Sea Takes Us*, Fourth Estate, 2007.

Moore, John Norton ed., *The Vietnam Debate: a fresh look at the arguments*, University Press of America, 1990.

Nguyen, Chi Thien, *Hoa Dia Nguc (The Flowers of Hell)*, To Hop Xuat Ban Mien Dong, Hoa Ky Publishers, Virginia, 2006.

Nguyen, Mau Lam, *Noi Lua (Fire Up)*, Que Me Publisher, 1988.

Nguyen, Nathalie Huynh Chau, *Memory Is Another Country – Women of the Vietnamese Diaspora*, Praeger, 2009.

Nha Ca, *Giai Khan So Cho Hue*, Thuong Yeu Publisher, Saigon, 1969.

Nha Ca (author), Olga Dror (translator), *Mourning Headband for Hue: An Account of the Battle for Hue, Vietnam 1968*, Indiana University Press, 2014.

Qiang Zhai, *China and the Vietnam Wars, 1950-1975*, The University of North Carolina Press, 2000.

United Nations High Commissioner for Refugees, *The State of The World's Refugees: Fifty Years of Humanitarian Action*, Oxford University Press, 2000.

Wong Alcoh Yahao, Vietnamese Graveyards In Terengganu, http://bidong.itgo.com/ [viewed 15 September 2016].

www.ingramcontent.com/pod-product-compliance
Lightning Source LLC
Chambersburg PA
CBHW050633300426
44112CB00012B/1784